BROWNIES, BLONDIES
and other traybakes

BROWNIES, BLONDIES
and other traybakes

65 delicious recipes for home-baked sweet treats

RYLAND PETERS & SMALL
LONDON • NEW YORK

Senior Designer Toni kay
Editor Alice Sambrook
Head of Production
 Patricia Harrington
Art Director Leslie Harrington
Editorial Director Julia Charles
Publisher Cindy Richards
Indexer Hilary Bird

First published in 2016 and
reissued in 2021 by
Ryland Peters & Small
20–21 Jockey's Fields
London WC1R 4BW
and
341 E 116th St
New York NY 10029

www.rylandpeters.com

Recipe collection compiled
by Alice Sambrook. Text © Amy Ruth
Finegold, Annie Rigg, Bea Vo, Carol
Hilker, Claire Burnet, Dan May, Hannah
Miles, Jordan Bourke, Julian Day, Laura
Washburn, Linda Collister, Liz Franklin,
Mickael Benichou, Nicola Graimes, Sarah
Randell, Shelagh Ryan, Victoria Glass,
Will Torrent and Ryland Peters & Small
2016. Design and photographs
© Ryland Peters & Small 2016.

ISBN: 978-1-78879-385-8

10 9 8 7 6 5 4 3

A CIP record for this book is available
from the British Library. US Library of
Congress CIP data has been applied for.

Printed and bound in China

Notes
* Both British (Metric) and American
(Imperial) are included in these recipes
for your convenience, however it is
important to work with one set of
measurements and not alternate
within a recipe.
* All eggs are medium (UK) or large
(US) unless specified as large, in which
case US extra-large should be used.
Recipes containing raw or partially
cooked eggs should not be served to
the very young, very old, anyone with
a compromised immune system or
pregnant women.
* Where a recipe calls for the grated zest
of citrus fruit, buy unwaxed fruit and
wash well before using. If you can only
find treated fruit, scrub well in warm
soapy water before using.
* Ovens should be preheated to the
specified temperatures. We recommend
using an oven thermometer. If using
a fan-assisted oven, adjust temperatures
according to the manufacturer's specific
instructions.

FSC
www.fsc.org

MIX
Paper from
responsible sources
FSC® C008047

Contents

Introduction

The quest for the elusive *best-ever* brownie is one that never ends, it can be sprung upon you at any moment – whether eaten in the corner of a cosy café, accompanying coffee at a friend's house, or attending an unassuming bake sale, a truly fabulous brownie is something you will find yourself lusting after for years to come. Likewise, blondies, the trendy younger sister of the brownie and the extended family of traybakes, are just as well-loved, and this genre of straightforward baking ensures goodies to suit every occasion. The bakes in this book are equally delicious consumed warm fresh from the oven with a cup of tea or coffee, packed in a box and eaten cold, or warmed through and served with cream, custard or ice cream as a dinner party dessert.

As the epitome of easy but delicious, throw-together bakes, brownies, blondies and traybakes are accessible to bakers of all levels. All you really need is a mixing bowl, a rectangular pan and a hot oven to create amazing treats.

Once you have mastered the basics you can choose to dress up your creations with different toppings and decorations to create something pretty. As with all baking, it pays to use the very best ingredients: fresh eggs, good-quality fruit and chocolate with a high cocoa percentage. You can also experiment with fancy chocolate that contains extra pre-added ffavourings such as coffee, orange or sea salt. This is a fabulous collection of recipes to ignite your baking inspiration, so get in the kitchen and rustle up one of these delightful bakes.

In the Sweet and Simple chapter find classics such as the Millionaire's Shortbread or Belgian Chocolate Blondie. In the Fabulously Fruity chapter try a zesty Chocolate, Ginger and Orange Slice or a Very Berry Cheesecake Brownie. Go Absolutely Nuts with a Pistachio Brownie or Hazelnut Praline Brownie in the chapter devoted to all things nutty. In Healthier and Wholesome find virtuous Muesli Bars and Carrot Oat Squares for those days when you need something a little lighter. The Little Kids and Big Kids chapter is bursting with fun ideas such as Brownie Pops and Whoopie Pies, which will delight kids and adults alike. Finally, discover luscious creations like the Butterscotch Blondie or Black Forest Brownies in the Deliciously Decadent chapter.

SWEET AND SIMPLE

Chocolate fudge brownies

The kind of disappointing, mealy brown cake served in some cafés as brownies is a long way from the real thing. A genuine brownie should first and foremost taste intensely of chocolate. There should be undertones of coffee and vanilla and it should be dark and nutty, with a fudge-like centre and a firm, slightly crispy outer surface. This easy recipe is intended to produce such classic brownies. To portion, refrigerate until chilled, then slice with a sharp knife.

3 eggs

220 g/1 cup plus 2 tablespoons caster/superfine sugar

300 g/10½ oz. dark/bittersweet chocolate, broken into pieces

220 g/2 sticks butter

2 teaspoons vanilla extract

1 tablespoon instant coffee granules

2 tablespoons water, boiling

70 g/½ cup self-raising/self-rising flour

100 g/⅔ cup chopped walnuts

a 34 x 20 x 3-cm/14 x 8 x 1¼-inch baking pan, greased and lined with baking parchment

Makes 20

Preheat the oven to 180°C (350°F) Gas 4.

Put the eggs and sugar in a large bowl. With a balloon whisk or a hand-held electric whisk, beat together until smooth, very thick and pale, and no sugar is left in the base of the bowl.

Melt the chocolate and butter in a heatproof bowl set over a pan of barely simmering water. Do not let the base of the bowl touch the water. Stir frequently until smooth and well mixed. Put the vanilla extract and coffee granules in a cup, add the boiling water and stir until dissolved and smooth. Add the melted chocolate and butter to the egg and sugar mixture, followed by the coffee infusion and stir to mix. Fold in the flour, then add the walnuts and gently stir through.

Spoon the mixture into the prepared baking pan and bake in the preheated oven for 35–40 minutes until just firm to the touch. Remove the brownies from the oven and leave to cool in the pan, then turn out onto a wire rack. They are best eaten warm or at room temperature but are easier to slice when chilled.

The brownies will keep in an airtight container at room temperature for 7–10 days. They are also good for home freezing.

If you are not a fan of white chocolate, you will still like these. If you are a fan of white chocolate, you will love these. The unique structure of white chocolate allows the batter to stay quite gooey even when cooked. For this recipe it is essential to have real white chocolate as opposed to 'white chocolate product', which will clump up and separate into an oily mess when melted with butter.

Belgian blondies

Preheat the oven to 170°C (325°F) Gas 3.

Put the chocolate in a medium bowl. Put the butter in a pan and melt until just boiling. Pour the butter immediately over the chocolate and stir with a wooden spoon until well combined and smooth.

Put the eggs, sugar and vanilla extract in a large mixing bowl and beat together using a hand-held electric whisk. Pour the warm chocolate mixture into the egg mixture and stir. Add the flour and salt and mix until just combined.

Transfer the mixture to the prepared brownie pan and bake in the preheated oven for 28–33 minutes. It should be golden brown on top and still gooey in the centre, so a wooden skewer test will not work.

Remove from the oven and leave to cool in the pan for 1 hour. Refrigerate for 2 hours. Remove the blondie from the pan and cut into 12 squares.

Tip: Make sure you use real, high-quality white chocolate and not white chocolate baking drops. White chocolate consists of milk, sugar and cocoa butter, while white baking drops are made of vegetable oil, weird flavouring, sugar and some type of milk product: a no-no in baking.

480 g/1 lb. good-quality white chocolate, chopped into pea-size pieces

320 g/2¾ sticks butter

2 eggs

250 g/1¼ cups caster/superfine sugar

1 teaspoon vanilla extract

250 g/1¾ cups plus 2 tablespoons plain/all-purpose flour

a pinch of salt

a 30 x 20 x 5-cm/12 x 8 x 2-inch baking pan, greased and lined with baking parchment

Makes 12

Bakewell slices

If you like Bakewell tart but have only ever eaten the commercially produced variety, you're in for a treat. No sign here of sickly sweet fondant icing or a neon-bright cherry on top – just a sweet pastry base, good raspberry jam/jelly and fragrant frangipane paste topped with almonds. It is excellent as a teatime treat or served warm with cream.

PASTRY BASE

200 g/1½ cups plus 2 tablespoons plain/all-purpose flour

50 g/⅓ cup ground almonds

75 g/⅓ cup caster/superfine sugar

160 g/11 tablespoons butter, at room temperature, cubed

1 egg yolk

150 g/⅔ cup raspberry jam/jelly

FILLING

130 g/9 tablespoons butter, softened

160 g/¾ cup caster/superfine sugar

4 eggs

260 g/1¾ cups ground almonds

40 g/⅓ cup flaked/slivered almonds, to decorate

a 34 x 20 x 3-cm/14 x 8 x 1¼-inch baking pan, greased

baking parchment

baking beans

Makes 12

Put the flour, ground almonds and sugar in a large bowl and stir until evenly mixed. Add the butter and use your fingertips to rub it into the mixture until the texture resembles breadcrumbs. Add the egg yolk and, still using your hands, mix and knead until the dough binds together into a tight, smooth ball.

Wrap the dough in clingfilm/plastic wrap and refrigerate for about 30 minutes until firm. Remove the pastry from the refrigerator and allow to rest at room temperature for 15 minutes before using.

Preheat the oven to 170°C (325°F) Gas 3.

On a lightly floured work surface, carefully roll out the pastry until about 5 mm/¼ inch thick and use it to line the baking pan. The pastry is fragile to handle but any gaps can be repaired using surplus pastry. Gently press along the sides and into the corners and trim off the excess pastry with a sharp knife. Prick the base in a few places with a fork and line the tart case with a sheet of baking parchment. Fill the tart case with baking beans and blind bake in the preheated oven for 15–20 minutes. Remove from the oven and set aside to cool. Leave the oven on.

Spread the raspberry jam/jelly evenly over the cooled pastry base.

To make the filling, cream together the butter and sugar in a large bowl until pale and fluffy. Add the eggs one at a time, beating after each addition. Add the ground almonds and whisk thoroughly.

Spoon the filling over the jam/jelly base and spread to the sides of the pan. Sprinkle the flaked/slivered almonds over the top and bake in the hot oven for 30–35 minutes or until the filling is golden on top and feels firm in the middle. Remove from the oven and leave to cool before cutting into 12 slices.

The slices will keep in an airtight container for 5–7 days.

Buttery carrot cake

Carrot cake is always a popular choice with mid-morning coffee. This version is spiced up with cinnamon, raisins and orange. The sweetened mascarpone topping has a lovely texture, less dense than the classic cream cheese. Orange zest is a simple but effective decoration, but you could always make the traditional little baby carrots out of coloured marzipan or fondant icing if you prefer.

250 g/2 sticks butter, softened

250 g/1¼ cups golden caster/granulated sugar, plus extra for dusting

4 eggs, beaten

300 g/2⅓ cups self-raising/self-rising flour

2 large carrots, peeled and grated

2 teaspoons ground cinnamon

grated zest and juice of 1 orange

50 g/⅓ cup sultanas/golden raisins

MASCARPONE TOPPING

50 g/3 tablespoons mascarpone

100 g/½ cup caster/superfine sugar

zest of 2 oranges, cut into fine slivers or shavings

a 20 x 30-cm/8 x 12-inch baking pan, greased

Makes 15

Preheat the oven to 180°C (350°F) Gas 4.

Cream together the butter and sugar in a large bowl until light and fluffy. Beat in the eggs a little at a time, until the mixture is smooth. You can add a little flour in between each addition if the mixture seems to be curdling.

Stir in the remaining flour, grated carrot, cinnamon and orange juice and zest. Add the sultanas/golden raisins and stir until everything is fully incorporated. Spoon the mixture into the prepared pan and bake for 35–40 minutes, until risen and golden. Dust with a little more sugar and leave to cool in the pan.

To make the topping, beat the mascarpone and sugar together. Cut the cake into squares and decorate with little dollops of the mascarpone mixture and a little orange zest.

Chocolate tiffin

A firm favourite with children, using good-quality chocolate, fruit and nuts means this tasty, no-bake cake is equally appealing to adults, too. Quick to make, it can be prepared in advance and is ideal for parties.

400 g/14 oz. digestive biscuits/ graham crackers

100 g/⅔ cup sultanas/golden raisins

70 g/½ cup roughly chopped pecans

60 g/½ cup chopped glacé/ candied cherries

70 g/½ cup dark/bittersweet chocolate chips or chunks

250 g/8½ oz. dark/bittersweet chocolate, roughly chopped

90 g/⅓ cup plus 1 tablespoon golden syrup/light corn syrup

70 g/4½ tablespoons butter

a 34 x 20 x 3-cm/14 x 8 x 1¼-inch baking pan, lined with baking parchment

Makes 18

Put the biscuits/crackers in a plastic bag and tap them with a rolling pin to break up into small pieces, but not crumbs. Put the pieces in a large bowl with the sultanas/golden raisins, pecans, cherries and chocolate chips and mix together with a wooden spoon.

Put the chopped chocolate in a heatproof bowl set over a pan of barely simmering water. Do not let the base of the bowl touch the water. Add the syrup and butter and mix together, stirring continuously, until melted and smooth. This can also be done in a microwave: heat for a few seconds, remove, stir and return to the microwave, repeating until fully melted.

Pour the melted chocolate mixture into the mixing bowl with the dry ingredients and mix until everything is well coated in chocolate.

Spoon the mixture into the prepared baking pan, spread level and press down firmly with the back of the spoon. Refrigerate and allow to harden completely, preferably overnight. To portion, slice using a sharp knife.

The tiffin will keep for 3–5 days in the refrigerator, or freeze for up to 2 months.

Flapjacks

330 g/3½ cups jumbo rolled oats

140 g/1½ cups medium rolled oats

100 g/½ cup dark muscovado/
    dark brown soft sugar

200 g/13 tablespoons butter

200 g/¾ cup golden syrup/light
    corn syrup

50 g/3 tablespoons glucose syrup
    or liquid glucose (optional)

*a 34 x 20 x 3-cm/14 x 8 x 1¼-inch
    baking pan, lined with baking
    parchment*

Makes 14–16

Wholesome and nourishing and packed with oats for slow-release energy, a chunk of flapjack will keep you going for hours. Simple, inexpensive and so easy to make, this is a great recipe to get children involved with baking.

Preheat the oven to 180°C (350°F) Gas 4.

In a large bowl, stir together the oats and sugar, crumbling any lumps of sugar with your fingers to ensure it is fully mixed.

In a pan set over medium heat, melt together the butter, golden syrup/light corn syrup and glucose syrup (if using). Do not allow to boil. Pour into the bowl with the oats and carefully stir together with a wooden spoon – stirring too vigorously at this stage has the effect of making the finished flapjack dense and you'll lose the nice open, crumbly texture.

Spoon the mixture into the prepared baking pan and gently level the top with a fork, easing the mixture along the edges and into the corners. Bake in the preheated oven for 25 minutes or until golden brown. Remove from the oven and leave to cool in the pan. The flapjack is quite soft at first but hardens as it cools. When completely cool, turn out of the pan onto a board and cut into 14–16 slices with a sharp serrated knife, using a sawing motion.

The flapjacks will keep in an airtight container for 7–10 days.

Millionaire's shortbread

SHORTBREAD

75 g/6 tablespoons caster/
    granulated sugar

150 g/10 tablespoons butter,
    softened

125 g/1 cup plain/all-purpose
    flour

100 g/¾ cup rice flour

a generous pinch of salt

2 teaspoons vanilla extract

**CARAMEL AND CHOCOLATE
TOPPING**

125 g/1 stick butter

75 g/6 tablespoons light
    muscovado/light brown soft
    sugar

25 g/1 tablespoon plus 2 teaspoons
    golden syrup/light corn syrup

1 tablespoon vanilla extract

a pinch of salt

1 x 379-g/14-oz. can (sweetened)
    condensed milk

200 g/6½ oz. dark/bittersweet
    chocolate, chopped

*a 20-cm/8-inch square loose-
    bottomed/springform cake pan,
    greased and lined with baking
    parchment*

Makes 16

Sticky, sweet and deliciously indulgent, this traybake can't fail to hit the spot. Shortbread dates back to Elizabethan-era Scotland, the millionaire layers of caramel and chocolate being a more recent addition, believed to have been introduced in the 19th century.

Preheat the oven to 150°C (300°F) Gas 2.

Cream together the sugar and butter in a large bowl until light and fluffy. Sift over the flours and mix together with the salt and vanilla extract until just combined. Do not overwork the dough or the shortbread will be tough.

Press the dough in the base of the cake pan with your fingers or using the back of a spoon and bake for 45–50 minutes. Leave to cool in the pan on a wire rack.

Meanwhile, make the caramel topping. Put all the ingredients, except for the condensed milk, into a pan and stir over a gentle heat until the butter has melted and the sugar has dissolved. Add the condensed milk and increase the heat, stirring frequently, being careful not to let the base of the mixture catch. Bring to the boil, still stirring every now and then, until the mixture has thickened and turned a deep golden colour. Remove from the heat and leave to cool slightly. Pour the warm caramel over the cooled shortbread base and leave to cool completely.

Melt the chocolate in a heatproof bowl set over a pan of barely simmering water. Do not let the base of the bowl touch the water. Once melted, leave to cool slightly before pouring the chocolate over the cold caramel. Leave to cool completely before pushing the base of the pan out and cutting into 16 squares to serve.

Lavender shortbread

Shortbread is the ultimate easy yet delicious traybake. The addition of gentle lavender makes this one the perfect sweet treat to accompany a pot of Earl Grey tea. Because there are so few ingredients, be sure to use the best of everything, including fine sea salt.

Preheat the oven to 150°C (300°F) Gas 2.

Whizz both the sugars, the lavender and salt in a stand mixer fitted with a paddle attachment (or rub with your fingertips) until the lavender buds are bruised and the sugars smell of lavender.

Beat the butter into the sugar mixture until well combined. Fold in the flour until just combined.

Transfer the mixture to the prepared baking pan and pat the dough down until well combined and level. Sprinkle sugar over the top.

Bake in the preheated oven for 40–55 minutes or until the top is golden brown and the edges shrink from the sides of the pan.

Remove from the oven and leave to cool in the pan for 10 minutes. Remove from the pan and cut into 24 squares.

70 g/⅓ cup caster/superfine sugar, plus extra for sprinkling

2 tablespoons icing/confectioners' sugar

½ teaspoon dried lavender buds

¼ teaspoon fine sea salt

350 g/3 sticks butter, slightly softened, cubed

350 g/2½ cups plain/all-purpose flour

a 30 x 20 x 5-cm/12 x 8 x 2-inch baking pan, lined with parchment paper

Makes 24

Parkin pieces

85 g/⅔ cup plain/all-purpose flour

85 g/¾ cup medium oatmeal

40 g/3 tablespoons dark muscovado/dark brown soft sugar

1 teaspoon ground ginger

¼ teaspoon grated nutmeg

½ teaspoon bicarbonate of/baking soda

65 g/½ stick butter

60 g/¼ cup golden syrup/light corn syrup

65 g/¼ cup black treacle/molasses

1 egg, lightly beaten

an 18 x 18-cm/7 x 7-inch baking pan, lined with baking parchment

Makes 9

A classic Northern British parkin uses half treacle/molasses and half golden syrup/light corn syrup, to give it a light colour and sweet taste. If you can resist long enough, it will get stickier and more delicious over time as the spices infuse, so is best baked a week in advance.

Preheat the oven to 170°C (325°F) Gas 3.

Put the flour, oatmeal, sugar, spices and bicarbonate of/baking soda in a large bowl and mix together with your fingertips until all the ingredients, especially the sugar, are thoroughly combined.

In a pan set over low heat, melt the butter, syrup and treacle/molasses together until fully liquid.

Slowly add the melted ingredients, the egg and 65 ml/¼ cup warm water to the dry ingredients, stirring rapidly all the time, until a smooth texture is obtained.

Pour the mixture into the prepared baking pan and bake in the preheated oven for 45 minutes or until the surface of the parkin springs back from finger pressure.

When the pan has cooled enough to be safely handled, turn out the parkin and allow to cool fully on a wire rack. Cut into 9 squares, wrap in clingfilm/plastic wrap and place in an airtight container. Store in a cool place (not refrigerated) for 24 hours or so before serving.

It will keep for up to 2 weeks in an airtight container.

Coffee blondies

Use a vegetable peeler to make piles of chocolate shavings to decorate these moreish cappuccino-like squares.

100 g/1 cup pecans

200 g/1 cup light muscovado/light brown soft sugar

175 g/1½ sticks butter

3 tablespoons instant coffee granules

1½ tablespoons boiling water

2 eggs, lightly beaten

250 g/2 cups plain/ all-purpose flour

2 teaspoons baking powder

a pinch of salt

100 g/⅔ cup dark/ bittersweet chocolate chips

COFFEE CREAM TOPPING

200 ml/¾ cup double/heavy cream

2 tablespoons icing/ confectioners' sugar

mixed chocolate shavings

chocolate-coated coffee beans

a 20 x 30-cm/8 x 12-inch baking pan, greased and lined with baking parchment

Makes 16–20

Preheat the oven to 170°C (325°F) Gas 3.

Tip the pecans onto a baking sheet and lightly toast in the preheated oven for 5 minutes. Roughly chop and leave to cool. Leave the oven on for the brownies.

Put the sugar and butter into a medium pan over low–medium heat and melt, stirring constantly. In a small bowl, dissolve the coffee granules in the boiling water. Stir two-thirds into the pan (reserve the rest for the topping). Remove from the heat, transfer the mixture to a bowl and leave to cool completely.

Stir the eggs and vanilla extract into the pan until smooth. Sift the flour, baking powder and salt into the pan and fold in until well mixed, then stir in the chocolate chips and pecans. Pour the mixture into the prepared baking pan, spread level and bake on the middle shelf of the preheated oven for about 25 minutes, or until just set in the middle and the top has formed a light crust. Remove from the oven and leave to cool completely in the pan. To decorate, whip the cream with the reserved coffee and sugar. Remove the brownies from the pan, cut into portions, top with a dollop of coffee cream and scatter chocolate shavings and coffee beans over the top.

Sticky toffee traybake with toffee fudge drizzle

175 g/1½ sticks butter, softened

125 g/⅔ cup dark muscovado/ dark brown soft sugar

150 g/scant ½ cup golden syrup/ light corn syrup

75 g/generous ¼ cup black treacle/ molasses

200 g/1½ cups self-raising/ self-rising flour

1 teaspoon vanilla extract

3 eggs

2 tablespoons double/heavy cream

2 balls stem ginger in syrup, drained and finely chopped

TOFFEE FUDGE TOPPING

50 g/3½ tablespoons butter

1 tablespoon of the syrup from the jar of stem ginger

2 tablespoons double/heavy cream

75 g/⅓ cup dark muscovado/dark brown soft sugar

40 g/⅓ cup icing/confectioners' sugar

a 20 x 30-cm/8 x 12-inch baking pan greased and lined with baking parchment

Serves 14

This indulgent traybake is perfect for a cold winter's day. Served warm with cream it would make a great dessert. You could try adding sultanas/golden raisins and use golden syrup/light corn syrup in the topping instead of the ginger. Both versions will vanish very quickly!

Preheat the oven to 180°C (350°F) Gas 4.

Put the butter, sugar, golden syrup/light corn syrup, treacle/molasses, flour, vanilla extract, eggs and double/heavy cream in large mixing bowl and beat until combined using a stand mixer or a hand-held electric whisk. Stir in the stem ginger.

Tip the mixture into the prepared pan and spread level with a spatula. Bake in the preheated oven for 25–30 minutes, or until risen and just set in the middle. Leave to cool completely in the pan.

To make the toffee fudge topping, put the butter, ginger syrup, cream and muscovado/dark brown soft sugar in a medium pan over low heat and leave until the butter has melted and the sugar dissolved. Remove the pan from the heat, sift in the icing sugar, then whisk it in.

Remove the cake from the pan and drizzle the topping over. Leave to set before cutting into 14 slices to serve.

FABULOUSLY FRUITY

Lemon squares

These look pretty as they are, lightly dusted with icing/confectioners' sugar, but you can top each square with a slice of fig or strawberry.

100 g/¾ cup plain/all-purpose flour

35 g/4 tablespoons icing/confectioners' sugar, plus extra for dusting

75 g/¾ stick butter, chilled and cubed

1–2 fresh figs, very thinly sliced, to decorate (optional)

LEMON LAYER

3 eggs

275 g/scant 1½ cups caster/superfine sugar

finely grated zest of 1 lemon

150 ml/1 cup freshly squeezed lemon juice (from 3–4 lemons)

50 g/generous ⅓ cup plain/all-purpose flour

an 18-cm/7-inch square baking pan, greased and lined with baking parchment

Makes 16

Preheat the oven to 180°C (350°F) Gas 4.

First prepare the baking pan. Place 2 wide strips of baking parchment from one side to the other of the pan so that they form a cross on the base – this will help you to lift the cake out of the pan when it is cooked. Place a square of baking parchment on top of the strips, as you would usually do to line the base of a pan.

Put the flour, icing/confectioners' sugar and butter in an electric mixer (or use a large mixing bowl and a hand-held electric whisk) and whizz until the mixture resembles breadcrumbs. Tip the mixture into the prepared pan and spread level with a spatula. Prick the base a few times with a fork. Bake in the preheated oven for 12–15 minutes, or until lightly golden. Reduce the oven temperature to 150°C (300°F) Gas 2.

To make the lemon layer, put the eggs, sugar and lemon zest in the electric mixer and beat for a minute or so. With the beaters still going, gradually pour in the lemon juice, then sift in the flour and mix to combine.

Tip the mixture on top of the baked base. Bake for 45 minutes, by which time the lemon layer will be set and the top slightly crusty. Leave to cool completely.

Run a sharp knife around the edges, then lift out of the pan. Lightly dust with icing/confectioners' sugar and cut into 16 squares.

Decorate with the thin slices of fig, if using.

Berries and white chocolate are a match made in heaven, and these squidgy squares are the perfect afternoon pick-you-up. If you prefer, you could add raspberries or even black cherries instead. The fruitier the better!

White chocolate and blueberry blondies

Preheat the oven to 170°C (325°F) Gas 3.

Cream together the butter and sugar until light and fluffy. Beat in the eggs, one at a time. If the mixture begins to curdle, add a tablespoon or two of the flour. Once all the eggs have been added, beat in the cooled melted chocolate. Fold in the remaining flour and salt, followed by the nuts (if using) and blueberries, until the batter is evenly studded.

Pour the batter into the prepared pan and bake in the preheated oven for 45–50 minutes, or until a skewer inserted into the middle comes out just clean. Leave to cool in the pan on top of a wire rack for 10 minutes, before turning out and cutting into 16 squares. These blondies are delicious eaten warm or cold.

250 g/8 oz. white chocolate, melted and cooled
250 g/2 sticks butter, softened
250 g/1¼ cups caster/granulated sugar
4 eggs
165 g/1⅓ cups plain/all-purpose flour
a pinch of salt
100 g/⅔ cup macadamia nuts, roughly chopped (optional)
150 g/1½ cups fresh blueberries

a 20 x 25-cm/8 x 10-inch cake pan, greased and lined with baking parchment

Makes 16

Apricot and almond brownies

Freshly baked apricots taste amazing, and when they're cooked on top of brownies they are even better. A scattering of toasted almonds complements the flavours perfectly.

225 g/8 oz. dark/bittersweet chocolate, chopped

150 g/1¼ sticks butter, cubed

125 g/1 cup flaked/slivered almonds

225 g/1 cup plus 2 tablespoons caster/superfine sugar

4 eggs

1 teaspoon vanilla extract

125 g/1 cup plain/all-purpose flour

a pinch of salt

8 fresh apricots, stoned/pitted and quartered

a 20 x 30-cm/8 x 12-inch baking pan, greased and lined with baking parchment

Makes 16–20

Preheat the oven to 170°C (325°F) Gas 3.

Melt the chocolate and butter in a heatproof bowl set over a pan of barely simmering water. Do not let the base of the bowl touch the water. Stir frequently until smooth. Leave to cool slightly.

Meanwhile, put two-thirds of the flaked/slivered almonds in a frying pan/skillet over low heat and dry-fry, stirring often, until toasted and golden.

In a separate bowl, lightly beat together the sugar, eggs and vanilla extract. Add the melted chocolate mixture and stir until combined. Sift the flour and salt into the bowl and fold in until well incorporated, then stir in the toasted almonds.

Pour the mixture into the prepared baking pan, spread level and arrange the quartered apricots on top. Scatter the remaining flaked/slivered almonds all over the brownies. Bake on the middle shelf of the preheated oven for 40 minutes, or until the brownies have set and the apricots are soft.

Remove from the oven and leave to cool completely in the pan before removing from the pan and cutting into portions to serve.

Banana and nutmeg custard brownies

These deliciously different brownies might just be the ones for you. A dark chocolate brownie base is topped with a sweet and creamy custard and sprinkled with nutmeg. It is always best to use overly ripe bananas when baking, as the texture needs to be soft enough to incorporate smoothly into the batter. A cup of tea paired with these and the stresses of the world may just fade away...

Preheat the oven to 180°C (350°F) Gas 4.

Melt the butter, sugar, chocolate and cocoa powder together in a heatproof bowl set over a pan of barely simmering water. Do not let the base of the bowl touch the water. Stir frequently until smooth and well mixed.

Remove from the heat and leave to cool slightly.

Stir in the eggs. Add the flour and baking powder and stir again until smooth. Add the mashed banana and mix well. Pour the mixture into the prepared pan.

For the custard layer, beat the mascarpone, egg yolks and sugar together until smooth. Drizzle the mixture randomly across the chocolate layer. Scatter the custard mixture with grated nutmeg. Bake for about 35 minutes, until firm but still slightly fudgy.

Leave to cool in the pan, then cut into squares.

20 g/4 teaspoons butter

450 g/2¼ cups caster/superfine sugar

50 g/1½ oz. dark/bittersweet chocolate

100 g/¾ cup cocoa powder

4 eggs, beaten

100 g/¾ cup plain/all-purpose flour

1 teaspoon baking powder

2 very ripe bananas, mashed

CUSTARD LAYER

250 g/1 cup mascarpone

4 egg yolks

100 g/½ cup caster/superfine sugar

freshly grated nutmeg

a 20 x 30-cm/8 x 12-inch baking pan, greased and lined with baking parchment

Makes 15

Chocolate, ginger and orange slices

This brownie has a proper dense, fudge-like texture with an added dimension
of orange and ginger, flavours that go beautifully with chocolate.

3 eggs

220 g/1 cup plus 2 tablespoons
   caster/granulated sugar

300 g/10 oz. dark/bittersweet
   chocolate, chopped

220 g/2 sticks butter

4½ teaspoons vanilla extract

1 tablespoon instant coffee
   granules

2 tablespoons boiling water

finely grated zest of 3 oranges

2 balls stem ginger in syrup,
   drained and finely chopped

2 teaspoons ground ginger

80 g/⅔ cup self-raising/self-rising
   flour

50 g/⅓ cup crystallized ginger,
   finely cubed

*a 34 x 20 x 3-cm/14 x 8 x 1¼-inch
   baking pan, greased and lined
   with baking parchment*

Makes 14–16

Preheat the oven to 180°C (350°F) Gas 4.

Put the eggs and sugar in a large bowl. With a balloon whisk or a hand-held electric whisk, beat together until smooth, very thick and pale, and no sugar is left in the base of the bowl.

Melt the chocolate and butter in a heatproof bowl set over a pan of barely simmering water. Do not let the base of the bowl touch the water. Stir frequently until smooth. Put the vanilla extract and coffee granules in a cup, add the boiling water and stir vigorously until dissolved. Add the melted chocolate and butter to the beaten egg and sugar mix, followed by the coffee infusion and the orange zest. Stir with a balloon whisk until smooth. Stir in the stem ginger. Sift together the ground ginger and flour, then gently stir into the bowl until well mixed. Spoon the mixture into the prepared baking pan, sprinkle the crystallized ginger evenly over the top and bake in the preheated oven for 35–40 minutes or until just firm to the touch.

Remove the brownies from the oven and leave to cool in the pan, then turn out onto a wire rack. They are best eaten warm or at room temperature but are easier to slice when chilled. To portion, refrigerate the brownies until chilled, then slice with a sharp knife. The brownies will keep in an airtight container at room temperature for 7–10 days.

Cherry marzipan streusel squares

100 g/¾ cup plain/all-purpose flour

50 g/3½ tablespoons butter, chilled and cubed

1 tablespoon icing/confectioners' sugar

5 tablespoons morello cherry jam/jelly

STREUSEL TOPPING

75 g/generous ½ cup plain/all-purpose flour

75 g/generous ⅓ cup caster/granulated sugar

25 g/2 tablespoons butter, softened and cubed

50 g/2 oz. marzipan, cubed

50 g/¼ cup natural glacé/candied cherries, chopped

50 g/⅓ cup flaked/slivered almonds

ALMOND LAYER

100 g/7 tablespoons butter, softened and cubed

75 g/generous ⅓ cup caster/superfine sugar

2 eggs, lightly beaten

100 g/1 cup ground almonds

25 g/3 tablespoons plain/all-purpose flour

an 18-cm/7-inch square loose-based baking pan, greased and lined with baking parchment

Makes 12

You can also make these divine bites with raspberry or plum jam/jelly.

For the pastry, put the flour, butter and sugar in an electric mixer and whizz until the mixture resembles breadcrumbs. Add 2 tablespoons cold water and whizz again. Add a few more drops of water, if needed, to bring together into a dough.

Tip the pastry out on a lightly floured work surface and roll out thinly and evenly. Trim the edges with a sharp knife to make a 19-cm/7½-inch square. Line the base of the baking pan with the pastry – it will come slightly up the inside of the pan all the way round. Refrigerate for 30 minutes.

Preheat the oven to 200°C (400°F) Gas 6.

To make the streusel topping, tip the flour and sugar into the electric mixer (or use a hand-held electric whisk) and whizz together. Add the butter and whizz until the mixture is crumbly. Tip into a bowl and stir in the marzipan, glacé/candied cherries and flaked/slivered almonds.

To make the almond layer, mix all the ingredients together in the electric mixer until amalgamated.

Spread the cherry jam/jelly on top of the chilled pastry base. Spoon blobs of the almond mixture on top of the jam and spread them out with a spatula. Scatter the streusel topping over the top. Put the pan on a baking sheet and bake in the preheated oven for 40 minutes, or until lightly golden. Cover with foil towards the end of cooking to prevent over-browning. Leave to cool in the pan before cutting into 12 squares to serve.

Summer fruit slice

250 g/1¾ cups plus 2 tablespoons plain/all-purpose flour

200 g/2 cups ground almonds

200 g/1¾ sticks butter

200 g/1 cup caster/granulated sugar

2 eggs

300 g/10½ oz. mixed summer berries, such as raspberries, strawberries and blackberries, plus extra to serve

a 20-cm/8-inch square baking pan, greased and lined with baking parchment

Makes 16

This slice has a fruity surprise sandwiched in the centre - a juicy layer of summer berries. Serve it in squares with an extra helping of fresh berries. A scoop of vanilla ice cream is also delicious. If fresh berries are out of season, you can use frozen fruit instead (bags of frozen mixed berries are nutritious and very convenient).

Preheat the oven to 180°C (350°F) Gas 4.

Put the flour, almonds, butter, sugar and eggs in a food processor and mix to a soft dough. Divide the mixture in half.

Press one half of the dough into the prepared baking pan. The easiest way to do this is to take a small handful of dough, flatten it slightly in your hand, then press it into the pan. Repeat to make an even layer about 1 cm/½ inch thick. Lightly press the summer berries into the dough in an even layer. Top the fruit with the remaining dough, covering it in an even layer using the method above.

Bake in the preheated oven for 35–40 minutes or until the top is a light golden colour. Remove from the oven and transfer to a wire rack to cool for 10 minutes.

To remove the cake from the pan, put a wire rack on top of the pan and carefully turn it over so the rack is on the bottom – the cake should slide out of the pan. Peel away the baking parchment lining, then turn the cake over. Cut into 16 squares and serve with berries.

Nectarine and blueberry traybake with lavender sugar

This traybake is packed full of juicy fruit. You can leave out the lavender if it isn't your thing and the nectarines can be swapped for peaches, a similar quantity of plums, apricots or even mixed berries. In any case, this traybake is best made and eaten on the same day.

3 eggs

200 g/1 cup caster/granulated sugar

175 g/1⅓ cups plus 1 tablespoon self-raising/self-rising flour, sifted

1 teaspoon baking powder

½ teaspoon vanilla extract

175 g/1½ sticks butter, softened and cubed

½ tablespoon dried lavender buds

3 ripe but firm nectarines

200 g/1½ cups fresh blueberries

1 tablespoon polenta (cornmeal)

LAVENDER SUGAR

½ tablespoon dried lavender buds

2 tablespoons caster/granulated sugar

grated zest of 1 lemon

a 20 x 33-cm/8 x 13-inch baking pan, greased and lined with baking parchment

Makes 14

Preheat the oven to 180°C (350°F) Gas 4.

Put the eggs, sugar, flour, baking powder, vanilla extract, butter and lavender in an electric mixer (or use a hand-held electric hand whisk) and beat together. Pit/stone the nectarines, chop them into bite-size pieces and carefully fold into the mixture along with the blueberries.

Dust the bottom of the prepared pan with the polenta (cornmeal) and a very small amount of flour. Spoon the mixture into the pan and spread it evenly with a spatula.

To make the lavender sugar, mix the ingredients together in a bowl, then scatter evenly over the traybake.

Bake in the preheated oven for 35 minutes, or until risen and golden. Leave to cool in the pan before cutting into 14 rectangles to serve.

Spiced pear cake

250 g/1¾ cups plus 2 tablespoons plain/all-purpose flour

1½ teaspoons baking powder

1 teaspoon bicarbonate of/baking soda

1½ teaspoons ground cinnamon

1½ teaspoons ground ginger

2 eggs

240 ml/1 cup whole milk

200 ml/scant 1 cup golden syrup/light corn syrup

35 g/2 tablespoons runny honey

125 g/1 stick butter

125 g/⅔ cup light muscovado/light brown soft sugar

400 g/1½ cups (about 2 large) peeled, cored and sliced pears

6 tablespoons fruit jam/jelly (apricot, apple or plum)

100 g/1 cup flaked/slivered almonds, toasted

a 25-cm/10-inch square baking pan, greased and lined with baking parchment

Makes 6–8

This is a lovely cake that you could serve cold with a cup of tea or coffee, or warm as an after-dinner dessert with custard or cream. Brushing the finished cake with warm jam/jelly helps to keep it moist and sticky.

Preheat the oven to 170°C (325°F) Gas 3.

Sift the flour, baking powder, bicarbonate of/baking soda, cinnamon and ginger into a large mixing bowl.

In a separate bowl, lightly beat the eggs and milk together.

Warm the syrup, honey and butter very gently in a pan set over a low heat. Stir in the sugar and keep on the heat until the butter and sugar melt together. Remove the pan from the heat and set aside to cool slightly.

Pour the warm syrup mixture into the bowl with the flour in and stir gently using a large, metal spoon. Add the beaten egg mixture and stir to combine.

Pour the mixture into the prepared cake pan and drop in the pear slices evenly over the surface – they should sink into the batter.

Bake in the preheated oven for 45–60 minutes or until a skewer inserted into the middle comes out clean, checking regularly after 40 minutes. If it looks as though the top is browning too quickly, cover with foil to stop it burning and return to the oven.

Meanwhile, melt the jam/jelly in a pan set over a medium heat.

Remove the cake from the oven and liberally brush with the warm jam/jelly. Sprinkle with flaked/slivered almonds and cut into 6–8 slices to serve.

Very berry cheesecake brownies

These brownies are a wonderful combination of light fruity cheesecake on a fudgy chocolate base. They are very rich but quite delicious served as a special dessert or even as mini sweet bites for a party.

Preheat the oven to 170°C (325°F) Gas 3.

To make the brownie base, melt the chocolate and butter in a heatproof bowl set over a pan of barely simmering water. Do not let the base of the bowl touch the water. Stir occasionally until smooth. Remove from the heat and leave to cool for a few minutes.

Beat the eggs and sugar together in a separate bowl. Fold in the rice flour and ground almonds. Add the melted chocolate mixture and gently fold it all together.

Pour the mixture into the prepared pan and tap on the work surface to ensure the mixture is spread level.

To make the cheesecake topping, beat the cream cheese and sugar together in a bowl using a wooden spoon or a hand-held electric whisk. Add the eggs and vanilla extract and mix in until you have a smooth consistency.

Pour the cheesecake mixture over the brownie base and push it into the corners with a palette knife or the back of a metal spoon. Push the berries into the cheesecake topping, covering as much or as little of the surface as you wish.

Bake in the preheated oven for about 40–45 minutes, or until risen, golden and firm around the edges, but still pale in the middle and with a slight wobble.

Leave to cool in the pan for at least 2 hours then transfer the pan to the refrigerator to chill fully.

Use the foil lining to lift the chilled brownies out onto a chopping board and cut into squares with a hot knife. You may want to wipe the knife clean between each cut as it will be messy and doing so will keep each brownie square looking neat.

The brownies will keep stored in an airtight container in the refrigerator for 4 days, but do bring them back to room temperature before eating.

Note: If preferred you can use 100 g/³⁄₄ cup of plain/all-purpose flour as an alternative to the rice flour and ground almonds.

200 g/7 oz. dark/bittersweet chocolate, chopped

150 g/1¼ sticks butter, chilled and cubed

3 eggs

150 g/³⁄₄ cup golden caster/ superfine sugar

60 g/½ cup fine rice flour

40 g/⅓ cup ground almonds

CHEESECAKE TOPPING

300 g/1½ cups full-fat cream cheese, at room temperature

100 g/½ cup golden caster/ superfine sugar

2 eggs, beaten

½ teaspoon vanilla extract

125 g/4½ oz. mixed fresh berries, such as raspberries, blueberries and blackberries

a 23-cm/9-inch square baking pan, base and sides lined with a single piece of foil

Makes 16

Chocolate fudge raspberry shortbread bars

125 g/1⅛ sticks butter, softened

50 g/¼ cup caster/granulated sugar

150 g/1 cup plus 2 tablespoons plain/all-purpose flour

CHOCOLATE TOPPING

400 ml/1¾ cups double/heavy cream

2 tablespoons icing/confectioners' sugar

400 g/15 oz. dark/bittersweet chocolate (70% cocoa solids), chopped

200 g/7 oz. fresh raspberries

a 20-cm/8-inch square baking pan, greased

Makes 21

This decadent number is quite rich but the tart fruitiness of the raspberries cuts through the dark/bittersweet chocolate nicely.

Preheat the oven to 190°C (375°F) Gas 5.

Cream together the butter and sugar in a stand mixer or using a hand-held electric whisk until pale and creamy. Tip in the flour and mix again for a few minutes to combine – the dough probably won't come together in a ball, but if you work it briefly with a wooden spoon and then your hands, it will come together. Tip into the prepared pan and press down firmly with the back of a spoon to make an even layer.

Prick the base a few times with a fork. Bake in the preheated oven for 20 minutes, or until lightly golden. Leave to cool.

To make the chocolate topping, bring the cream and icing/confectioners' sugar slowly to the boil in a pan. Put the chocolate pieces in a heatproof bowl. As soon as the cream begins to bubble, remove from the heat and pour into the bowl with the chocolate. Gently whisk together until the chocolate has melted and the mixture is smooth. Stir the raspberries into the chocolate mixture, then pour it over the cooled biscuit base. Leave to cool completely, then refrigerate for 3 hours, or until set. Cut into 21 bars with a sharp knife to serve.

Cranberry and white chocolate blondies

175 g/1½ sticks butter, cubed

175 g/1⅓ cups white chocolate, finely chopped

125 g/⅔ cup caster/granulated sugar

75 g/generous ⅓ cup light muscovado/light brown soft sugar

3 eggs

1 teaspoon vanilla extract

125 g/⅔ cup plain/all-purpose flour

75 g/¾ cup ground almonds

½ teaspoon baking powder

a pinch of salt

75 g/½ cup white chocolate chips

100 g/⅔ cup dried cranberries

50 g/⅔ cup flaked/slivered almonds

TO DECORATE

75–100 g/½–¾ cup white chocolate, chopped

1 tablespoon freeze-dried cranberry powder (optional)

20 x 30-cm/8 x 12-inch baking pan, greased and lined with baking parchment

Makes 16-20

These fancy, fruity blondies contain ground almonds, which really help to keep the texture soft and chewy, just like a proper blondie should be, and cranberries to cut through the sweetness of the white chocolate. Finished with an extra drizzle of white chocolate and sprinkled with freeze-dried cranberries, these make an irresistible dessert and can be kept in the refrigerator overnight.

Preheat the oven to 180°C (350°F) Gas 4.

Melt the chocolate and butter in a heatproof bowl set over a pan of barely simmering water. Do not let the base of the bowl touch the water. Stir occasionally until smooth.

Tip the caster/granulated and light muscovado/light brown soft sugar into a large mixing bowl with the eggs. Beat with a hand-held electric whisk for about 5 minutes, until pale, light and the mixture holds a ribbon trail. Add the vanilla and whisk again. Pour the butter and white chocolate mixture into the bowl and mix briefly to combine. Sift in the plain/all-purpose flour, ground almonds, baking powder and salt, and mix gently. Fold in the white chocolate chips and dried cranberries.

Spoon the mixture into the prepared baking pan, spread level and scatter with flaked/slivered almonds.

Bake on the middle shelf of the preheated oven for 30 minutes, until the top has a light crust but the middle is still soft to the touch. Remove from the oven and set aside to cool.

Melt the remaining white chocolate in a heatproof bowl set over a pan of simmering water. Stir until smooth, remove from the heat and cool slightly.

Drizzle the melted white chocolate over the top of the blondies, from a height. Set aside for 10 minutes and then sprinkle with freeze-dried cranberry powder, if using. Cut into squares to serve.

The blondies will keep in an airtight container for up to 1 week.

Coconut, apricot and lime slices

125 g/1⅛ sticks butter, softened

50 g/¼ cup Demerara sugar

150 g/1 cup plus 2 tablespoons plain/all-purpose flour

450 g/16 oz. ready-to-eat dried apricots, finely chopped

grated zest and freshly squeezed juice of 3 limes

COCONUT TOPPING

2 eggs

160 ml/5½ oz. coconut cream

50 g/¼ cup caster/superfine sugar

125 g/1½ cups desiccated/shredded coconut

a 20 x 30-cm/8 x 12-inch baking pan, greased

Makes 14

Here is a tropical version of a classic coconut slice. The traditional version has raspberry jam beneath the coconut topping, but these are all the better for their juicy apricot layer.

Preheat the oven to 180°C (350°F) Gas 4.

Put the butter and sugar in an electric mixer and beat for 3–4 minutes, or until pale and creamy. Tip in the flour and mix again for a few minutes to combine.

Tip the mixture into the prepared pan and press down firmly with the back of a spoon to make an even layer. Prick the base a few times with a fork. Bake in the preheated oven for 15–20 minutes, or until lightly golden. Leave the oven on.

Meanwhile, put the apricots and lime zest and juice in a medium pan with 4 tablespoons cold water and bring to simmering point. Gently cook, covered, for 8–10 minutes, or until soft and mushy. Add another tablespoon of water if the mixture seems too dry as it simmers. Leave the apricots to cool slightly, then transfer to a food processor and whizz to a thick purée.

To make the coconut topping, lightly beat the eggs in the electric mixer, then add the coconut cream, sugar and desiccated/shredded coconut and mix to combine.

Spread the apricot purée on top of the baked base and top with the coconut mixture, spreading it evenly. Bake for 40–45 minutes, or until golden. Leave to cool completely before cutting into 14 slices.

ABSOLUTELY NUTS

Chocolate and hazelnut brownies

The chocolate brownie is said to have been created at the Palmer House Kitchen Hotel in Chicago at the request of Bertha Palmer, to be served at the Columbian Exposition World Fair in 1893. Despite only gaining popularity in the early 20th century, it feels like brownies have been part of American food culture forever. This version has added hazelnuts and the overall flavour may remind you of your favourite chocolate spread.

Preheat the oven to 160°C (325°F) Gas 3.

Melt the chocolate and butter in a heatproof bowl set over a pan of barely simmering water. Do not let the base of the bowl touch the water. Stir frequently until smooth and well mixed.

In the meantime, whisk together the sugars, eggs and salt in a large bowl until light and creamy. Whisk in the chocolate mixture and vanilla extract.

Sift over the flour, cocoa, baking powder, bicarbonate of/baking soda and mix together. Fold in the chocolate chips and nuts and pour the mixture into the prepared cake pan. Level the top with a palette knife and bake for 35–40 minutes. A skewer inserted into the middle should still have a little stickiness left on it.

Leave to cool in the cake pan on a wire rack before turning out and cutting into 16 equal squares.

250 g/8 oz. dark/bittersweet chocolate, chopped

250 g/2 sticks butter

125 g/½ cup plus 2 tablespoons light muscovado/light brown soft sugar

125 g/½ cup plus 2 tablespoons caster/granulated sugar

4 eggs, beaten

¼ teaspoon salt

2 teaspoons vanilla extract

75 g/⅔ cup rice flour

50 g/⅓ cup plus 1 tablespoon cocoa powder

½ teaspoon baking powder

½ teaspoon bicarbonate of/baking soda

100 g/3½ oz. milk/semisweet chocolate chips

75 g/½ cup chopped hazelnuts

a 20-cm/8-inch square cake pan, greased and lined with baking parchment

Makes 16

This blondie recipe is packed with rich and buttery macadamia nuts. For best results use nuts from a freshly opened package as they spoil quickly.

Macadamia and white chocolate blondies

Preheat the oven to 180°C (350°F) Gas 4.

Melt the chocolate and butter in a heatproof bowl set over a pan of barely simmering water. Do not let the base of the bowl touch the water. Stir occasionally until combined and smooth.

Remove the bowl from the pan and stir in the sugar with a wooden spoon – don't worry if the mixture looks curdled. Gradually stir in the beaten eggs, then the vanilla extract and beat for a minute until the mixture becomes thick and glossy.

Sift the flour and baking powder directly onto the mixture and stir in. When thoroughly combined stir in two-thirds of the chopped nuts, and the chopped white chocolate.

Transfer the mixture to the prepared pan, spread evenly and level the surface. Scatter the remaining macadamia nuts over the top.

Bake in the preheated oven for about 20–25 minutes until light golden brown and a skewer inserted in the middle comes out just clean. Remove from the oven.

Leave to cool in the pan before removing and cutting into 20 pieces. Store in an airtight container and eat within 4 days.

175 g/6 oz. white chocolate, chopped

115 g/1 stick butter, cubed

100 g/½ cup caster/superfine sugar

2 eggs, lightly beaten

½ teaspoon vanilla extract

130 g/1 cup plain/all-purpose flour

½ teaspoon baking powder

150 g/1¼ cup macadamia nuts, roughly chopped

100 g/3½ oz. white chocolate, roughly chopped or white chocolate chips

a 23-cm/9-inch square baking pan, greased and lined with baking parchment

Makes 20

Bonjour brownies

250 g/8 oz. dark/bittersweet chocolate (55% cocoa solids), chopped

100 g/7 tablespoons butter, at room temperature and chopped

120 g/generous ½ cup caster/superfine sugar

2 eggs

60 ml/¼ cup whole milk

120 g/1 scant cup plain/all-purpose flour

25 g/¼ cup ground almonds

1 teaspoon baking powder

1 vanilla pod/bean

20 g/2 tablespoons macadamia nuts

20 g/2 tablespoons walnuts, chopped

a 20-cm/8-inch square baking pan, greased and and lined with baking parchment

Makes 6-8

This is a classic recipe with added macadamias and walnuts. It is very important to cream the butter well, as it will add softness to the brownie while both varieties of nuts add some excellent crunch. The perfect match for a cup of strong espresso.

Preheat the oven to 190°C (375°F) Gas 5.

Melt the chocolate in a heatproof bowl set over a pan of barely simmering water. Do not let the base of the bowl touch the water. Stir occasionally until smooth. Remove from the heat.

Put the butter in a bowl and beat with a wooden spoon until very soft. Beat in the sugar until well incorporated, then beat in one egg at a time. Add the milk and stir in. Add the flour, almonds and baking powder and beat in. Split the vanilla pod/bean lengthways and scrape the seeds out into the bowl. Pour the melted chocolate in too and mix everything together well. Finally, stir in the macadamias and walnuts.

Spoon the mixture into the prepared baking pan, spread level with a spatula and bake in the preheated oven for about 20 minutes. Allow the brownies to cool in the pan for a few minutes, then turn out onto a wire rack to cool completely.

Serve at room temperature, cut into equal portions.

Cinnamon pecan blondies

This is a deliciously moist and chewy little blondie packed with pecan halves, rather than pieces, and flavoured with a touch of warming cinnamon.

100 g/7 tablespoons butter

300 g/1½ cups light muscovado/ light brown soft sugar

½ teaspoon ground cinnamon

2 eggs, lightly beaten

150 g/1 cup plus 2 tablespoons plain/all-purpose flour

1 teaspoon baking powder

100 g/generous ¾ cup pecan halves

icing/confectioners' sugar, for dusting

a 23-cm/9-inch square baking pan, greased and lined with baking parchment

Makes 30

Preheat the oven to 180°C (350°F) Gas 4.

Put the butter in a large pan set over low heat and melt gently. Add the sugar and cinnamon and stir until smooth and melted. Remove the pan from the heat and set aside to cool for a couple of minutes.

Use a wooden spoon to stir in the eggs, beating the mixture well until thoroughly combined. Sift the flour and baking powder onto the mixture, then stir in. Mix in the pecans then transfer the mixture to the prepared pan, spreading level with a spatula.

Bake in the preheated oven for about 25 minutes until golden brown and a skewer inserted in the middle comes out just clean. Remove from the oven.

Leave to cool in the pan for 5 minutes before removing and transferring to a wire rack. Wait until the brownies are completely cold before dusting liberally with icing/confectioners' sugar and cutting into 30 small pieces. Store in an airtight container and eat within 4 days.

Pistachio brownies

These brownies are dense, delicious and a doddle to make! The striking green of the pistachios looks pretty against the dark/bittersweet chocolate.

250 g/2 sticks butter

500 g/2½ cups caster/superfine sugar

100 g/¾ cup cocoa powder

50 g/1½ oz. dark/bittersweet chocolate, chopped

4 eggs, beaten

100 g/¾ cup self-raising/self-rising flour

100 g/⅔ cup unsalted pistachios, roughly chopped

a 20 x 30-cm/8 x 12-inch baking pan, greased and lined with baking parchment

Makes 15

Preheat the oven to 180°C (350°F) Gas 4.

Put the butter, sugar, cocoa powder and dark/bittersweet chocolate in a large heatproof bowl set over a pan of barely simmering water. Do not let the base of the bowl touch the water. Stir occasionally until the butter and chocolate have melted and the sugar has dissolved. Remove from the heat and leave to cool slightly.

Beat in the eggs, and then fold in the flour. Stir in the pistachios.

Spoon the mixture into the prepared pan and bake for about 40 minutes, until firm but still slightly fudgy.

Leave the brownies to cool in the pan, then cut into squares to serve.

Store any leftover brownies in an airtight container.

Fudgy dark chocolate and almond traybake

250 g/2 sticks softened butter

350 g/1¾ cups caster/superfine sugar

6 eggs, beaten

150 g/1 cup plus 2 tablespoons plain/all-purpose flour

150 g/1⅓ cups ground almonds

1 teaspoon almond essence

FUDGE TOPPING

180 g/scant 1 cup caster/granulated sugar

100 g/7 tablespoons butter

250 g/8 oz. dark/bittersweet chocolate, chopped

150 ml/⅔ cup evaporated milk

a 20 x 30-cm/8 x 12-inch baking pan, greased and lined with baking parchment

Makes 15

Like most traybakes, this one is quite simple to make, but the end result is really quite indulgent. You could try adding a little orange zest to the chocolate topping for an extra dimension that would work really well with the almond flavour. This cake would also go nicely with a cup of refreshing green tea to cut through the sweetness.

Preheat the oven to 180°C (350°F) Gas 4.

Cream together the butter and sugar together until light and fluffy. Add the eggs a little at a time until the mixture is smooth (you may have to add a little flour in between each addition to prevent curdling). Stir in the remaining flour, ground almonds and almond essence. Spoon into the prepared pan and bake for about 50 minutes, or until risen and golden. Leave to cool in the pan.

In the meantime, make the fudge topping. Put all the ingredients into a pan and heat until the sugar has dissolved and the butter and chocolate have melted. Simmer over gentle heat for 3–4 minutes, until the mixture thickens. Beat for 2–3 minutes until glossy, then refrigerate until cold.

Spread the topping over the cold cake. Cut into squares to serve.

Extra-nutty brownies

- 100 g/3½ oz. dark/bittersweet chocolate, chopped
- 115 g/1 stick butter
- 200 g/1 cup light muscovado/light brown soft sugar
- ½ teaspoon vanilla extract
- 2 eggs, lightly beaten
- 100 g/¾ cup plain/all-purpose flour
- 2 tablespoons unsweetened cocoa powder
- 200 g/1¾ cups walnut pieces

FUDGE TOPPING
- 50 g/1¾ oz. dark/bittersweet chocolate, chopped
- 50 g/3½ tablespoons butter
- 2 tablespoons whole milk
- 2 tablespoons unsweetened cocoa powder
- 100 g/¾ cup icing/confectioners' sugar

a 23-cm/9-inch square baking pan, greased and lined with baking parchment

Makes 20

Walnuts have a creamy, bittersweet taste that contrasts well with the sweetness of the brownie mixture. Here, there is a high proportion of walnuts to mixture, plus a fudgy topping. For a deeper flavour, toast the nuts for 10 minutes in the oven before adding to both the brownie mixture and topping.

Preheat the oven to 180°C (350°F) Gas 4.

Melt the chocolate and butter in a heatproof bowl set over a pan of barely simmering water. Do not let the base of the bowl touch the water. Stir occasionally until smooth.

Remove the bowl from the pan and stir in the sugar and vanilla extract. Add the eggs and use a wooden spoon or hand-held electric whisk to beat well until the mixture comes together as a smooth batter. Sift the flour and cocoa directly into the bowl and stir in. When combined, stir in the nuts (reserving about 50 g/1¾ oz. to top). Transfer the mixture to the prepared pan and spread level with a spatula.

Bake in the preheated oven for about 15 minutes or until just firm to the touch. Remove the pan from the oven. Leave to cool in the pan before carefully removing.

To make the topping, melt the chocolate and butter as above. Remove the bowl from the pan and stir in the milk. Sift the cocoa and icing/confectioners' sugar into the bowl and mix in. When the topping is thick and smooth, spread it over the cooled brownie. Push the reserved walnut pieces into the topping to finish.

Once the topping is firm, cut into 20 pieces to serve. Store in an airtight container and eat within 4 days.

These blondies have a double hit with melted white chocolate in the batter as well as white chocolate chips scattered throughout.

Double white chocolate and pecan blondies

75 g/¾ cup pecans

75 g/2½ oz. white chocolate, chopped

175 g/1½ cups plain/all-purpose flour

1 teaspoon baking powder

2 tablespoons malted milk powder

a pinch of salt

125 g/1 stick softened butter

175 g/¾ cup plus 2 tablespoons caster/granulated sugar

2 eggs, lightly beaten

1 teaspoon vanilla extract

75 g/½ cup white chocolate chips

a 20-cm/8-inch square baking pan, greased and lined with greased baking parchment

Makes 16

Preheat the oven to 170°C (325°F) Gas 3.

Tip the pecans onto a baking sheet and lightly toast in the preheated oven for 5 minutes. Roughly chop and leave to cool. Leave the oven on for the brownies.

Melt the chocolate in a heatproof bowl set over a pan of barely simmering water. Do not let the base of the bowl touch the water. Stir occasionally until smooth.

Sift together the flour, baking powder, milk powder and salt.

In a separate bowl, cream together the butter and sugar until pale and light. Gradually add the eggs, beating well after each addition. Stir in the vanilla extract. Add the melted chocolate and stir until combined. Fold the sifted dry ingredients into the bowl until well incorporated, then stir in the chocolate chips and pecans.

Spoon the mixture into the prepared baking pan, spread level and bake on the middle shelf of the preheated oven for 25–30 minutes, or until the brownies are golden and just cooked.

Remove from the oven and leave to cool completely in the pan before removing from the pan and cutting into 16 squares to serve.

Hazelnut praline brownies

PRALINE

150 g/¾ cup caster/superfine sugar

100 g/⅔ cup blanched hazelnuts

DEEP DARK CHOCOLATE BROWNIE

225 g/8 oz. dark/bittersweet chocolate, chopped

150 g/10 tablespoons butter, cubed

125 g/½ cup plus 1 tablespoon sugar

125 g/½ cup plus 1 tablespoon light muscovado/light brown sugar

4 eggs, lightly beaten

1 teaspoon vanilla extract

125 g/1 cup plain/all-purpose flour

a pinch of salt

TO DECORATE

1 quantity Ganache Topping (page 25)

100 g/½ cup caster/superfine sugar

100 g/⅔ cup blanched hazelnuts, lightly toasted

vanilla ice cream, to serve

a baking sheet, lightly oiled with sunflower oil

a 20-cm/8-inch square baking pan, greased and lined with greased baking parchment

Makes 12-16

If you don't want to make praline for these brownies, make the base recipe using chocolate that has praline pieces already added to it.

Make the praline first. Put the sugar and 1 tablespoon water in a small, heavy-based pan over low heat and let the sugar dissolve without stirring. Raise the heat and continue to cook for about 2–4 minutes until the sugar turns a deep amber colour. Quickly tip the hazelnuts into the pan and stir to coat evenly in the caramel. Spoon the mixture out onto the oiled baking sheet and leave to cool completely. When cold, blitz in a food processor until finely chopped. Re-oil the baking sheet and set aside.

Next, make the deep dark chocolate mix. Preheat the oven to 170°C (325°F) Gas 3.

Put the chocolate and butter in a heatproof bowl set over a pan of barely simmering water. Do not let the base of the bowl touch the water. Stir until smooth and thoroughly combined. Leave to cool slightly. Add both the sugars and mix well. Add the eggs one at a time, beating well after each addition. Stir in the vanilla extract. Sift the flour and salt into the bowl and stir until smooth.

Fold half of the chopped praline into the mixture. Spoon the mixture into the prepared baking pan, spread level with a spatula and bake on the middle shelf of the preheated oven for 20–25 minutes. Remove from the oven and leave to cool completely in the pan.

To decorate, prepare the Chocolate Ganache according to the recipe on page 25, then stir in 2 tablespoons of the chopped praline. Refrigerate until thick enough to spread.

Put the sugar and 1 tablespoon water in a small, heavy-based pan over low heat and let the sugar dissolve completely.

Bring to the boil, then cook until the syrup turns to an amber-coloured caramel. Remove from the heat and plunge the bottom of the pan into a sink of cold water. Quickly tip the hazelnuts into the pan and stir to coat evenly in the caramel. Using a fork, remove the hazelnuts from the caramel so that the caramel leaves long tails and place the nuts on the oiled baking sheet. Leave to harden.

Cut the brownies into diamonds or squares and spread the Chocolate Ganache on each one. Top with some caramelized hazelnuts and serve with ice cream and leftover praline scattered over the top.

Honey, toasted pine nut and pumpkin seed flapjacks with chocolate topping

Vary the dried fruit you use in these flapjacks according to what you have handy. They are a hit with children and adults alike.

Preheat the oven to 180°C (350°F) Gas 4.

Spread the pine nuts and pumpkin seeds on a baking sheet and toast in the preheated oven for 5 minutes, or until lightly golden. Leave to cool, then roughly chop. Leave the oven on.

Gently heat the butter, sugar and honey together in a small pan until melted, stirring every now and then. Remove the pan from the heat and leave to cool slightly.

Tip the dried fruit and oats into a large mixing bowl. Add the salt and the chopped pine nuts and seeds. Pour in the warm butter mixture and mix well.

Tip the mixture into the prepared baking pan and press down firmly with the back of a spoon to make an even layer. Bake in the preheated oven for 30 minutes, or until lightly golden.

Meanwhile, melt the chocolate in a heatproof bowl set over a pan of barely simmering water. Pour over the flapjack, then leave to cool completely.

Remove the flapjack from the pan and cut into 24 bars.

3 tablespoons pine nuts

2 tablespoons pumpkin seeds

175 g/1½ sticks butter

100 g/½ cup light muscovado/
light brown soft sugar

3 tablespoons runny honey

100 g/⅔ cup dried sour cherries or
cranberries, or chopped ready-
to-eat dried apricots, pears,
peaches or prunes, or a mixture

250 g/2½ cups rolled oats

a pinch of salt

200 g/7 oz. milk/semisweet
chocolate broken into pieces

*a 20-cm/8-inch square, loose-based
baking pan, greased and lined
with baking parchment*

Makes 24

HEALTHIER AND WHOLESOME

Apricot ffax oat bars

150 g/1½ cups rolled oats

60 g/½ cup chopped walnuts

65 g/½ cup plain/all-purpose flour (plus ½ teaspoon xanthan gum if using gluten-free plain/all-purpose flour)

170 g/½ cup brown rice syrup

25 g/⅛ cup dark muscovado/dark brown soft sugar

100 ml/⅓ cup melted butter

1 teaspoon vanilla extract

100 g/½ cup chopped dried apricots

25 g/¼ cup milled flaxseeds

a pinch of salt

1 egg, beaten

150 g/½ cup apricot preserve

an 18 x 28-cm/7 x 11-inch baking pan, greased and lined with baking parchment

Makes 12

This is a great afternoon treat that showcases apricots. If you can find them, Turkish dried apricots are the ones to use; they have a lovely meaty consistency that makes for a great bite!

Preheat the oven to 150°C (300°F) Gas 2.

Pulse the oats in a food processor, then put them in a large mixing bowl with the chopped walnuts and flour. Stir well, then pour the oat mixture onto a baking sheet. Toast in the preheated oven for 15 minutes, or until golden brown. Remove from the oven and set aside to cool. Leave the oven on.

Melt the rice syrup, sugar, butter, xanthan gum (if using) and vanilla in a small pan set over a medium heat. Bring the mixture to the boil and then quickly turn down the heat and simmer for a few minutes. Remove from the heat and set aside to cool slightly.

Return the cooled toasted oat mixture to the mixing bowl and add the chopped apricots, flaxseeds and a pinch of salt to the bowl. Toss to mix everything together. Then, add the syrup mixture. Mix together, then add the beaten egg. Make sure everything is mixed evenly.

Press down half the mixture in the prepared baking pan and spread level with a spatula or back of a wooden spoon until it is even and firmly packed. Then spread a layer of apricot preserve across the oat mixture and finally, spread the remaining oat mixture on top.

Bake in the preheated oven for 30 minutes. Remove from the oven and cool completely before cutting into even bars.

Shortcuts are always handy when cooking around a busy schedule. Because the granola is pre-made here, this tasty tray requires only assembly, and a bit of patience while the bars stick together!

Ginger cashew granola bars

Mix the granola, cashews, ginger and crisped rice cereal together in a large mixing bowl. Add the almond butter, rice syrup and oil and mix well so everything is well-coated.

Press the sticky batter into the pan and put in the refrigerator to set for at least 3 hours. Remove and cut into bars before serving.

Variation: Candied citrus peel is a great alternative to crystallized ginger in this recipe and gives the bars a tropical burst of tangy citrus flavour.

200 g/1¾ cups plain store-bought granola

60 g/½ cup well-chopped cashews

40 g/¼ cup well-chopped crystallized ginger

80 g/1 cup crisped rice cereal

50 g/¼ cup almond butter

115 g/⅓ cup brown rice syrup

1 tablespoon vegetable oil

a 20-cm/8-inch square baking pan, greased and lined with baking parchment

Makes 12

Carrot oat squares

A good carrot cake is hard to beat. Here, a recipe for just such a cake has been transformed so it doesn't feel like such a guilty pleasure.

150 g/1¼ cups plain/all-purpose flour (plus 1 teaspoon xanthan gum if using gluten-free plain/all-purpose flour)

100 g/1 cup rolled oats

110 g/½ cup light muscovado/light brown soft sugar

1 teaspoon bicarbonate of/baking soda

½ teaspoon baking powder

1 teaspoon ground cinnamon

½ teaspoon ground nutmeg

a pinch of salt

25 g/¼ cup chopped walnuts

35 g/¼ cup (dark) raisins

115 g/⅓ cup butter, melted

1 egg

210 ml/¾ cup apple purée/sauce

½ teaspoon vanilla extract

4 medium carrots, peeled and grated

a 20 x 28-cm/8 x 11-inch baking pan, greased and lined with baking parchment

Makes 10

Preheat the oven to 180°C (350°F) Gas 4.

Mix together the flour, oats, sugar, bicarbonate of/baking soda, baking powder, cinnamon, nutmeg and salt in a large mixing bowl. Add the walnuts and raisins and set aside.

In a separate bowl whisk together the xanthan gum (if using), melted butter, egg, apple purée/sauce and vanilla. Stir in the grated carrots, then mix the wet mixture into the dry.

Pour the batter into the prepared baking pan and bake in the preheated oven for 30 minutes, or until a knife comes out clean. Remove from the oven and set aside to cool completely before cutting into equal squares.

Cocoa energy bars

75 g/½ cup sliced dried figs

150 g/1½ cup rolled oats

35 g/¼ cup oat flour

25 g/⅓ cup chopped almonds

120 g/1½ cups crisped rice cereal

50 g/⅓ cup dark/bittersweet chocolate chips

3 tablespoons brown sugar

4 tablespoons cocoa powder

50 g/¼ cup almond butter

60 ml/¼ cup coconut oil

115 g/⅓ cup brown rice syrup

80 ml/⅓ cup almond milk

1 teaspoon vanilla extract

an 18 x 28-cm/7 x 11-inch baking pan, greased and lined with baking parchment

Makes 12

Energy and protein bars are everywhere you look and it's easy to understand why. They are the perfect snack for when you're on the go and need to curb hunger pangs. These are made with unsweetened cocoa powder for a chocolate fix and almonds for added protein.

Preheat the oven to 180°C (350°F) Gas 4.

Pulse the figs and oats together in a food processor and transfer the mixture to a large mixing bowl. Add the flour, almonds, crisped rice cereal, chocolate chips, sugar and cocoa powder and mix well. Set aside.

Melt the almond butter, coconut oil, rice syrup, almond milk and vanilla in a small pan set over a medium heat. Pour over the oat mixture and mix well so all the ingredients are well-coated.

Pour the bar mixture into the prepared baking pan and bake in the preheated oven for 30 minutes. Remove from the oven and set aside to cool completely before cutting into equal bars.

Maggie's muesli bars

These wholesome and tasty bars were invented to sustain hundreds of fundraisers on an all-night hike through London. Made with 2 types of oats for slow-release energy and packed with superfoods like dried apricots, goji berries and cranberries, these yummy cereal bars certainly fitted the bill.

Preheat the oven to 160°C (325°F) Gas 3.

Put the oats, sugar, dried fruit, sunflower seeds, nuts and coconut into a large bowl and mix with a wooden spoon.

In a pan set over low heat, melt together the butter, golden syrup/corn syrup, glucose syrup and vanilla extract, stirring continuously. Alternatively, melt them in short bursts in a microwave, checking and stirring regularly. Pour the melted ingredients over the dry mixture in the bowl and fold together with the wooden spoon.

Spoon the mixture into the prepared baking pan and press the mixture down firmly and evenly using a large metal spoon. Bake in the preheated oven for 35 minutes.

Remove from the oven and allow to cool. When completely cool, turn out of the pan onto a board and cut into 14–16 slices with a sharp serrated knife, using a sawing motion.

The muesli bars will keep in an airtight container at room temperature for 7–10 days.

Tip: Glucose syrup, or liquid glucose, is not essential in this recipe, but it helps give a nice gooey finished texture – if you can't find it, increase the quantity of golden syrup/light corn syrup by the same amount instead.

135 g/1⅓ cups jumbo rolled oats

135 g/1⅓ cups medium rolled oats

70 g/⅓ cup packed dark muscovado/ dark brown soft sugar

50 g/⅓ cup chopped dried apricots

35 g/¼ cup dried cranberries

35 g/¼ cup pitted and chopped Medjool dates

35 g/¼ cup raisins

35 g/¼ cup dried goji berries

50 g/⅓ cup sunflower seeds

35 g/¼ cup roughly chopped pecans

35g/¼ cup roughly chopped walnuts

35 g/⅓ cup desiccated/shredded coconut

200 g/1¾ sticks butter

70 g/⅓ cup golden syrup/light corn syrup

40 g/3 tablespoons glucose syrup (or liquid glucose – see Tip left)

1 teaspoon vanilla extract

34 x 20 x 3-cm/14 x 8 x 1¼-inch baking pan, greased and lined with baking parchment

Makes 14–16

Apple, fig and nut bars

Bars such as these could be described as a bake that falls somewhere between a tart and soft cookie. This filling is slightly reminiscent of fig-centred cookies but the apples make it lighter. Good for brunch, teatime or cake sales, or serve warm with ice cream for dessert.

2 large tart apples, such as Granny Smith, peeled, cored and finely chopped

2 tablespoons runny honey

2 tablespoons fresh orange juice

2 tablespoons apple juice or water

250 g/1⅔ cups dried figs, finely chopped

375 g/2¾ cups cups plain/ all-purpose flour

145 g/⅔ cup light muscovado/ light brown soft sugar

250 g/2¼ sticks butter, cubed

a good pinch of fine sea salt

½ teaspoon ground cinnamon

125 g/generous 1 cup pecans, hazelnuts, walnuts or almonds, finely chopped

a 33 x 23-cm/14 x 9-inch baking pan, greased and lined with baking parchment

Makes 16

Preheat the oven to 190°C (375°F) Gas 5.

In a large pan, combine the apples, honey, orange and apple juices. Set over low heat, cover and simmer gently, stirring occasionally, until tender, about 10–15 minutes. Use a wooden spoon to help mash the apple pieces. Add the figs and continue simmering, uncovered, until the figs are soft, about 5 minutes. If necessary, add more apple juice or water if the mixture seems too thick, and use a wooden spoon to mash to a coarse purée. Remove from the heat and set aside to cool.

In a food processor, combine the flour, sugar, butter, salt and cinnamon. Pulse to obtain coarse crumbs. Alternatively, blend in a bowl with a pastry cutter, if you have one, or use a palette knife, then rub in using your fingers to obtain coarse crumbs.

Press half the flour mixture into the bottom of the prepared baking dish. Spread the apple and fig mixture over the top in an even layer. Add the nuts to the remaining flour mixture and, using your fingertips, crumble the mixture over the apples in an even layer.

Bake in the preheated oven until browned, about 30–40 minutes. Leave to cool in the baking pan, then cut into bars. The bars will keep in an airtight container at room temperature for 7–10 days.

Orange-zest brownies

Everyone loves a good sticky, chewy chocolate brownie and although they are usually the ultimate in decadent home baking, this recipe is completely guilt-free – no processed sugar (well, hardly any), wheat or dairy. Happily, they are still delicious and indulgent-tasting.

225 g/7½ oz. dark/bittersweet chocolate, at least 70% cocoa solids (there is a tiny amount of sugar in the ingredients of dark/bittersweet chocolate. If you want no sugar at all you can buy sugar-free dark/bittersweet chocolate in health stores), chopped

110 g/1 cup rice flour

70 g/½ cup plus 1 tablespoon unsweetened cocoa powder

½ teaspoon baking powder

½ teaspoon sea salt

225 g/7 oz. dairy-free butter, such as sunflower or soy spread

170 g/¾ cup coconut palm sugar or xylitol

2 eggs

2 egg yolks

grated zest of 1 orange

100 g/⅔ cup pecans, lightly roasted

an 18-cm/7-inch square baking pan, greased and lined with baking parchment

Makes 10–12

Preheat the oven to 180°C (350°F) Gas 4.

Melt the chocolate in a heatproof bowl set over a pan of barely simmering water. Do not let the base of the bowl touch the water. Stir occasionally until smooth.

Sift the flour, cocoa powder, baking powder and salt into a bowl. In another bowl, beat the butter with the sugar until pale and fluffy. Slowly mix in the eggs and egg yolks, then the melted chocolate and orange zest. Finally, stir in the sifted ingredients and pecans. As the melted chocolate cools, the mixture becomes increasingly stiff and difficult to mix. Don't be tempted to add more liquid, as this is what makes these brownies so decadently chewy and dense in texture. If you have a food mixer it makes the job a little easier.

Spoon the mixture into the prepared baking pan and, with the back of a metal spoon, level the top, dipping the spoon into hot water every now and again to prevent it from sticking. Bake in the preheated oven for 25–30 minutes, depending on your oven and the thickness of your brownie. A skewer should come out with a bit of the wet mixture still on it, as the brownie will firm up once it has cooled completely and the chocolate sets. Once cool, cut into small squares, as it is very rich. Then devour!

These hearty bars, packed with nuts, seeds and dried fruit, are perfect for a quick energy fix. They are ideal for lunchboxes or as after-school treats, and contain plenty of natural goodness. You can omit some of the nuts, seeds or fruit, doubling up the quantities of others if you want to customize the recipe. Lexia raisins are extra-large Muscatel raisins and well worth looking out for.

Coconut and pumpkin power bars

100 g/7 tablespoons butter

50 g/¼ cup extra virgin coconut oil

150 g/¾ cup caster/granulated sugar

3 tablespoons golden syrup/light corn syrup

80 g/generous ½ cup gluten-free self-raising/self-rising flour OR 100 g/¾ cup gluten-free all-purpose baking flour plus 1 teaspoon baking powder and ⅛ teaspoon xanthan gum

2 eggs, beaten

150 g/2 cups desiccated/shredded coconut

100 g/1 cup unsalted pistachios

60 g/½ cup pumpkin seeds

60 g/½ cup sunflower seeds

60 g/½ cup pine nuts

150 g/1 cup raisins or sultanas/golden raisins

a 30 x 20-cm/12 x 8-inch deep-sided baking pan, greased and lined with baking parchment

Makes 14

Preheat the oven to 180°C (350°F) Gas 4.

Put the butter, coconut oil, sugar and syrup in a large pan and heat until the butter has melted. Take off the heat and leave to cool slightly.

Sift the flour into a mixing bowl and add all the remaining ingredients. Stir with a wooden spoon until everything is well mixed together. Pour in the cooled butter mixture and mix together.

Tip the mixture into the prepared pan and press down using the back of a spoon. Bake in the preheated oven for 20–25 minutes, until the top is golden brown and the mixture feels firm to the touch. Leave to cool completely in the pan then tip out and cut into bars to serve.

These bars will keep in an airtight container at room temperature for up to 5 days.

Flourless sticky brownies

300 g/10½ oz. dark/bittersweet
   chocolate, chopped

225 g/2 sticks butter, cubed

3 large eggs

200 g/1 cup plus 2 tablespoons
   light muscovado/light brown
   soft sugar

75 g/¾ cup ground almonds

1 teaspoon baking powder

100 g/1 cup walnut pieces

vanilla ice cream, to serve
   (optional)

a 23-cm/9-inch square baking pan,
greased and lined with baking
parchment

Makes 24

Many people want a good brownie recipe without flour, and this one
is quite wonderful. It is incredibly rich and sticky, and is perfect served
with a scoop of vanilla ice cream. As with many chocolate cakes, it is
at its best made a day in advance.

Preheat the oven to 180°C (350°F) Gas 4.

Melt the chocolate and butter in a heatproof bowl set over a pan of barely
simmering water. Do not let the base of the bowl touch the water. Stir occasionally
until smooth. Remove the bowl from the heat and set aside until needed.

Put the eggs and sugar in a mixing bowl and use a stand mixer or hand-held
electric whisk to whisk until very pale, thick and mousse-like in texture.

Using a large metal spoon, fold in the melted chocolate mixture. Combine the
ground almonds with the baking powder and mix in, followed by the walnuts.

Transfer the mixture to the prepared pan and spread level with a spatula. Bake
in the preheated oven for about 40 minutes until just firm to touch and a skewer
inserted in the centre comes out clean. Remove the pan from the oven.

Leave to cool completely in the pan before cutting into 24 pieces, or if possible,
wrap the entire brownie in foil or baking parchment and leave for a day before
cutting. Serve with ice cream, if liked. They will keep in an airtight container at
room temperature for 5 days.

LITTLE KIDS AND BIG KIDS

Peanut butter and jelly brownies

Peanut butter and jam/jelly are a common and much-loved sandwich filling, but take away the bread, add some chocolate, swirl it all together and it's a new brownie classic.

125 g/4 oz. dark/bittersweet chocolate, chopped

100 g/7 tablespoons butter, cubed

175 g/¾ cup plus 1 tablespoon caster/granulated sugar

3 eggs

100 g/¾ cup plus 1 tablespoon plain/all-purpose flour

a pinch of salt

4 generous tablespoons raspberry jam/jelly

PEANUT BUTTER SWIRL

75 g/⅓ cup cream cheese

1 egg, lightly beaten

1 teaspoon vanilla extract

100 g/½ cup caster/superfine sugar

150 g/⅔ cup smooth peanut butter

a 20 x 30-cm/8 x 12-inch baking pan, greased and lined with baking parchment

Makes 16–20

Preheat the oven to 170°C (325°F) Gas 3.

Make the peanut butter swirl first. Tip all the ingredients into a bowl and beat until smooth. Set aside.

Melt the chocolate and butter in a heatproof bowl set over a pan of barely simmering water. Do not let the base of the bowl touch the water. Stir occasionally until smooth. Leave to cool slightly.

In a separate bowl, whisk the sugar and eggs for 2–3 minutes until light and foamy. Add the melted chocolate mixture and stir until combined. Sift the flour and salt into the bowl and fold in until well incorporated.

Spoon two-thirds of the brownie mixture into the prepared baking pan and spread level with the back of a spoon. Dot one-third of the peanut butter mixture and all of the raspberry jam/jelly over the brownie. Spoon over the remaining brownie mixture, then the remaining peanut mixture in equal spoonfuls. Using a round-bladed knife, swirl the mixtures together to create a marbled effect. Tap the pan on the work surface to level the mixture and bake on the middle shelf of the preheated oven for about 20–25 minutes.

Remove from the oven and leave to cool completely in the pan before removing from the pan and cutting into portions to serve.

Looking somewhat like a lunar landscape, these squares should be generously topped with whichever chocolatey malted milk treats take your fancy.

Malted milk chocolate traybake

Preheat the oven to 170°C (325°F) Gas 3.

Tip the walnuts onto a baking sheet and lightly toast in the preheated oven for 5 minutes. Roughly chop and leave to cool. Leave the oven on for the brownies.

Sift together the flour, baking powder, bicarbonate of/baking soda, milk powder and salt.

In a separate bowl, cream together the butter and sugar until pale and light. Gradually add the eggs, beating well after each addition. Stir in the vanilla extract.

Fold the dry ingredients into the bowl until well incorporated, then stir in the halved malted milk balls and walnuts.

Spoon the mixture into the prepared baking pan, spread level and bake on the middle shelf of the preheated oven for 20–25 minutes, or until well risen and golden brown.

Remove from the oven and leave to cool completely in the pan.

Meanwhile, prepare the milk chocolate topping: tip the chocolates into a small, heatproof bowl. Heat the cream and syrup in a small pan until only just boiling. Pour it over the chopped chocolates, add the butter and leave to melt. Stir until smooth, then leave to thicken slightly before using.

Remove the cold brownie from the pan. Spread the milk chocolate topping evenly over it, then cut into 16 squares. Decorate with malted milk balls and chocolate sprinkles.

75 g/¾ cup walnuts

175 g/1½ cups plain/all-purpose flour

¼ teaspoon baking powder

¼ teaspoon bicarbonate of/baking soda

2 generous tablespoons malted milk powder

a pinch of salt

175 g/1½ sticks butter, softened

225 g/1 cup light muscovado/light brown soft sugar

3 eggs, lightly beaten

2 teaspoons vanilla extract

75 g/2½ oz. milk-chocolate-coated malted milk balls, halved

milk/semisweet- and white-chocolate-coated malted milk balls and assorted chocolate sprinkles, to decorate

MILK CHOCOLATE TOPPING

125 g/4 oz. dark/bittersweet chocolate (54–68% cocoa solids), finely chopped

125 g/4 oz. milk/semisweet chocolate, finely chopped

175 ml/⅔ cup double/heavy cream

1 tablespoon maple syrup or golden syrup/light corn syrup

125 g/1 stick softened butter, diced

a 23-cm/9-inch square baking pan, greased and lined with baking parchment

Makes 16

Chocolate marshmallow brownies

These irresistible brownies are best enjoyed while still warm if you want to fully experience the marshmallows melting into the gooey richness of the brownies.

112 g/½ cup butter

50 g/2 oz. dark/bittersweet chocolate (minimum 75% cocoa solids), chopped

200 g/1 cup caster/granulated sugar

2 eggs

1 teaspoon vanilla extract

60 g/½ cup plain/all-purpose flour

¼ teaspoon fine salt

1 teaspoon baking powder

25 g/1 oz. mini marshmallows (or large ones quartered)

a 20-cm/8-inch square baking pan, greased and lined with baking parchment

Makes 20

Preheat the oven to 175°C (340°F) Gas 4.

Melt the chocolate and butter in a heatproof bowl set over a pan of barely simmering water. Do not let the base of the bowl touch the water. Stir occasionally until smooth. Remove from the heat and let cool a little. Stir in the sugar, eggs and vanilla extract. Beat in the flour, salt and baking powder.

Spread half of the batter into the prepared baking pan. Add three quarters of the marshmallows.

Pour the other half of the brownie mixture over the chopped marshmallows and top with the rest of the marshmallows.

Bake in the preheated oven for 25–30 minutes, or until slightly springy in the middle. Leave to cool in the pan before removing and cutting into squares to serve.

Mint chocolate chip brownies

Keep a lookout for red and white peppermint candies to top these minty brownies. At Christmas time, you could decorate them with striped candy canes.

First, make the brownies. Preheat the oven to 170°C (325°F) Gas 3.

If you're adding nuts, tip them onto a baking sheet and lightly toast in the preheated oven for 5 minutes. Roughly chop and leave to cool. Leave the oven on for the brownies.

Melt the chocolate and butter in a heatproof bowl set over a pan of barely simmering water. Do not let the base of the bowl touch the water. Stir occasionally until smooth. Leave to cool slightly. In a separate bowl, whisk the sugar, eggs and peppermint extract with a balloon whisk until pale and thick. Add the melted chocolate mixture and stir until combined. Sift the flour, cocoa powder and salt into the bowl and fold in until well incorporated, then stir in all the chocolate chips and nuts (if using). Spoon the mixture into the prepared baking pan, spread level with a spatula and bake on the middle shelf of the preheated oven for about 25 minutes, or until the top has formed a light crust.

Remove from the oven and leave to cool completely in the pan.

Meanwhile, to make the mint buttercream, sift the icing/confectioners' sugar into a mixing bowl, add the soft butter and beat until smooth, pale and light. Add the peppermint extract and mix until combined.

Remove the cold brownie from the pan. Spread the buttercream in an even layer over the top and refrigerate until firm.

To make the chocolate glaze, melt the chocolate and syrup in a heatproof bowl set over a pan of barely simmering water. Do not let the base of the bowl touch the water. Stir occasionally until smooth. Remove from the heat and leave to cool and thicken slightly before using.

Spread the glaze over the top of the mint buttercream and refrigerate until set.

Cut the brownies into portions using a long, hot knife (this will ensure the knife glides neatly through the glaze and buttercream).

Decorate with the red and white peppermint candies.

100 g/1 cup walnuts or pecans (optional)

200 g/6½ oz. dark/bittersweet chocolate, chopped

175 g/1½ sticks butter, cubed

250 g/1¼ cups caster/granulated sugar

4 eggs

1 teaspoon peppermint extract

125 g/1 cup plain/all-purpose flour

2 tablespoons cocoa powder

a pinch of salt

75 g/½ cup milk/semisweet chocolate chips

75 g/½ cup white chocolate chips

MINT BUTTERCREAM

225 g/1¾ cups icing/confectioners' sugar

125 g/1 stick butter, softened

1 teaspoon peppermint extract

CHOCOLATE GLAZE

125 g/4 oz. dark/bittersweet chocolate, chopped

1 tablespoon golden syrup/light corn syrup

red and white peppermint candies, to decorate

a 23-cm/9-inch square baking pan, greased and lined with baking parchment

Makes 16

Rocky road popcorn slice

This delicious chocolate tiffin slice is packed with light popcorn, juicy cherries and chewy marshmallows. With milk/semisweet, dark/bittersweet and white chocolate, these tiny morsels are a chocoholic's dream. You only need to serve small squares as the slice is very rich.

Heat the oil in a large lidded pan with a few popcorn kernels in the pan. When you hear the kernels pop, carefully tip in the rest of the kernels. Shake the pan over the heat until the popping stops. Take care when lifting the lid as any unpopped kernels may still pop from the heat of the pan.

Tip the popcorn into a bowl, removing any unpopped kernels as you go.

In a heavy-based frying pan/skillet, dry roast the desiccated/shredded coconut, stirring all the time, until it starts to colour and give off a nutty aroma. Tip onto a plate and set aside to cool.

Melt the milk/semisweet and dark/bittersweet chocolate and butter in a large heatproof bowl set over a pan of barely simmering water, making sure that the base of the bowl does not touch the water. Stir the mixture to melt any lumps then remove the bowl from the pan, taking care as it will be hot, and leave to cool for about 10 minutes.

Add the popcorn, toasted coconut, marshmallows and cherries to the cooled chocolate mixture and stir well so that everything is evenly coated. Spoon the mixture into the prepared pan and press out flat with the back of a spoon.

For the topping, melt the white chocolate in a heatproof bowl set over a pan of barely simmering water, and drizzle over the top of the tiffin slice. Decorate with sugar sprinkles, if using. Chill in the fridge for 2 hours until set, then cut into 24 small squares and serve.

1 tablespoon sunflower or vegetable oil

30 g/2 tablespoons popcorn kernels

30 g/1 oz. long soft desiccated/shredded coconut

100 g/3½ oz. milk/semisweet chocolate, broken into pieces

100 g/3½ oz. dark/bittersweet chocolate, broken into pieces

65 g/4½ tablespoons butter

100 g/2 cups mini marshmallows (or large ones quartered)

150 g/5 oz. (about 1 cup) glacé/candied cherries

TOPPING

75 g/2½ oz. white chocolate

sugar sprinkles (optional)

an 18 x 28-cm/7 x 11-inch baking pan, greased and lined with baking parchment

Makes 24

Fudge crumble brownies

Baked in a muffin pan and filled and topped with vanilla fudge, these cute mini-brownies benefit from being made with the best crumbly fudge you can find.

Preheat the oven to 170°C (325°F) Gas 3.

Grease the insides of 10 of the muffin cups and line the base of each with a disc of greased baking parchment. Lightly dust with flour and tip out the excess.

Melt the chocolate and butter in a heatproof bowl set over a pan of barely simmering water. Do not let the base of the bowl touch the water. Stir until smooth and thoroughly combined. Leave to cool slightly.

In a separate bowl, whisk the sugars, eggs and vanilla extract for 2–3 minutes until light and foamy. Add the melted chocolate mixture and stir until combined. Sift the flour, baking powder and salt into the bowl and fold in until well mixed, then stir in the chopped fudge.

Divide the mixture between the prepared muffin cups and bake on the middle shelf of the preheated oven for 15 minutes, or until firm and well risen. Remove from the oven and leave to cool in the pan for 2 minutes, then loosen the edges of each brownie with a small palette knife. Tip the brownies out onto a wire rack and leave until completely cold before decorating.

Meanwhile, to make the fudge topping, put all the ingredients together in a small pan over gentle heat. Stir until melted and smooth, then leave to cool and thicken slightly before using.

Spoon the topping over each brownie, allowing it to drizzle down the sides. Scatter with chopped fudge and leave to set before serving.

175 g/6 oz. dark/bittersweet chocolate, chopped

125 g/1 stick butter, cubed, plus extra for greasing

100 g/½ cup sugar

50 g/¼ cup light muscovado/ light brown soft sugar

2 eggs

1 teaspoon vanilla extract

100 g/¾ cup plus 1 tablespoon plain/all-purpose flour, plus extra for dusting

½ teaspoon baking powder

a pinch of salt

50 g/2 oz. vanilla fudge chopped, plus extra to decorate

FUDGE TOPPING

125 g/4 oz. dark/bittersweet chocolate, finely chopped

100 ml/⅓ cup double/heavy cream

2–3 tablespoons maple syrup

a 12-cup muffin pan

Makes 10

Crackling brownie French fries

240 g/8½ oz. dark/bittersweet
chocolate, chopped

100 g/7 tablespoons butter,
at room temperature

120 g/⅔ cup caster/granulated
sugar

2 eggs

60 ml/¼ cup low-fat/
semi-skimmed milk

120 g/1 scant cup plain/
all-purpose flour

25 g/¼ cup ground almonds

1 teaspoon baking powder

1 vanilla pod/bean

2 bags of popping candy,
plus extra to serve

chocolate hazelnut spread, to serve

*a 20-cm/8-inch square baking pan,
greased and lined with baking
parchment*

Serves 6–8

This clever idea has the wow factor and is perfect for surprising dinner guests! Popping candy adds crackle inside the brownie, then if you cut it into large French fries, you can dip them in chocolate hazelnut spread and finish with more popping candy. American brownies meet French fries - c'est cool!

Preheat the oven to 190°C (375°F) Gas 5.

Melt the chocolate in a heatproof bowl set over a pan of barely simmering water. Do not let the base of the bowl touch the water. Stir occasionally until smooth. Remove from the heat.

Put the butter in a bowl and beat with a wooden spoon until very soft. Beat in the sugar until well incorporated and creamy, then beat in one egg at a time. Add the milk and stir in. Add the flour, almonds and baking powder and beat in. Split the vanilla pod/bean lengthways and scrape the seeds out into the bowl. Pour the melted chocolate in and add the popping candy. Mix everything together well.

Spoon the mixture into the prepared baking pan, spread level with a spatula and bake in the preheated oven for about 15–20 minutes. Allow to cool in the pan for a few minutes, then turn out onto a wire rack to cool completely.

Cut up the brownie into fat fries and serve with chocolate hazelnut spread for dipping in and extra popping candy for sprinkling over.

75 g/2½ oz. dark/bittersweet chocolate, chopped

75 g/5 tablespoons butter, cubed

275 g/2 generous cups plain/all-purpose flour

2 tablespoons cocoa powder

1 teaspoon baking powder

1½ teaspoons bicarbonate of/baking soda

a pinch of salt

125 g/⅔ cup light muscovado/light brown soft sugar

75 g/⅓ cup caster/granulated sugar

1 egg, lightly beaten

125 ml/½ cup sour cream, at room temperature

WHITE CHOCOLATE BUTTERCREAM

100 g/3½ oz. white chocolate, chopped

½ teaspoon vanilla extract

100 g/7 tablespoons butter, softened

150 g/1 cup icing/confectioners' sugar, sifted

CHOCOLATE GLAZE

100 g/3½ oz. dark/bittersweet chocolate, finely chopped

75 g/2½ oz. milk/semisweet chocolate, finely chopped

1 tablespoon sunflower oil

½–1 tablespoon golden syrup/light corn syrup

sugar sprinkles, to decorate

2 large baking sheets, lined with baking parchment

a piping bag, fitted with a star-shaped nozzle/tip

Makes 12

These started life as whoopie pies, but somewhere along the way they became more fudgy and rich. Definitely not just for the kids...

Brownie whoopie pies

Preheat the oven to 170°C (325°F) Gas 3.

Melt the chocolate and butter in a heatproof bowl set over a pan of barely simmering water. Do not let the base of the bowl touch the water. Stir occasionally until smooth. Leave to cool slightly.

Sift together the flour, cocoa powder, baking powder, bicarbonate of/baking soda and salt. In a large bowl, whisk together the sugars, egg and sour cream. Add the melted chocolate mixture and stir until combined. Finally, fold the sifted dry ingredients and 5 tablespoons boiling water into the bowl until well incorporated. Spoon 24 evenly sized dollops onto the prepared baking sheets, leaving plenty of space between each one. Bake on the middle shelf of the preheated oven for about 10–12 minutes. Leave to cool on the baking sheets for 3 minutes, then transfer to a wire rack until cold.

Meanwhile, prepare the white chocolate buttercream and chocolate glaze. For the buttercream, tip the chocolate into a heatproof bowl set over a pan of barely simmering water. Do not let the base of the bowl touch the water. Leave until melted and smooth, then leave to cool slightly. In a separate bowl, beat together the butter and sugar until pale and light. Add the vanilla extract and melted chocolate and beat until smooth.

To make the chocolate glaze, tip all the ingredients into a heatproof bowl set over a pan of barely simmering water. Do not let the base of the bowl touch the water. Stir occasionally until the chocolate has melted and the glaze is smooth. Remove from the heat and leave to cool and thicken slightly before using.

Spoon the buttercream into the prepared piping bag. Pipe a generous amount over half of the brownie whoppers. Sandwich with the remaining whoppers.

Spoon the glaze over the tops of the whoppers, decorate with sprinkles and leave to set before serving.

Millionairejacks

Two very special British traybakes merged into one, these millionaire's flapjacks combine the buttery, syrup-drenched oats of flapjacks with the caramel and chocolate topping of millionaire's shortbread. Sticky and sweet, with a pleasing chewiness, this fusion is extremely moreish. Consider yourself warned.

150 g/¾ cup light muscovado/
light brown soft sugar

150 g/10 tablespoons softened
butter

2 tablespoons golden syrup/
light corn syrup

200 g/1½ cups rolled oats

a pinch of salt

CARAMEL LAYER

125 g/1 stick butter

75 g/⅓ cup light muscovado/
light brown soft sugar

25 g/2 tablespoons golden syrup/
light corn syrup

1 tablespoon vanilla extract

a pinch of salt

1 x 379-g/14-oz. can sweetened
condensed milk

CHOCOLATE TOPPING

200 g/6½ oz. dark/bittersweet
chocolate, chopped

*a 20-cm/8-inch loose-bottomed
square baking pan, greased and
lined with baking parchment*

Makes 8

Preheat the oven to 150°C (300°F) Gas 2.

Start by making the flapjack. Melt together the sugar, butter and golden syrup/light corn syrup over a gentle heat, stirring all the time. Take the pan off the heat and stir in the oats and salt until fully combined and coated.

Spoon the flapjack mixture into the prepared pan and press it level with the back of a spoon. Bake for 35–40 minutes. Leave to cool in the pan on top of a wire rack.

Meanwhile, make the caramel layer. Put all the ingredients, except the sweetened condensed milk, into a pan and stir over a gentle heat until the butter has melted and the sugar has dissolved. Add the condensed milk and increase the heat, stirring frequently, and being careful not to let the base of the mixture catch. Bring to the boil, still stirring every now and then, until the mixture has thickened and turned a deep golden colour. Take the pan off the heat and leave to cool slightly.

Pour the warm caramel over the cooled flapjack base and leave to cool completely.

Put the chocolate in a heatproof bowl set over a pan of barely simmering water. Do not let the base of the bowl touch the water. Stir occasionally until the chocolate has melted and leave to cool slightly before pouring the chocolate over the cold caramel. Leave to cool completely before pushing the base of the pan out and cutting the millionaire flapjack into 8 bars.

Brookies

If you can't decide whether to bake brownies or cookies, why not make both? In this recipe, the two mixtures are combined to make one big cookie – or is it a brownie?

Make the cookie dough first. Sift together the flour, bicarbonate of/baking soda and salt. In a separate bowl, cream together the butter and sugars until pale and light. Gradually add the egg, beating well after each addition. Stir in the vanilla extract. Fold the sifted dry ingredients into the bowl until well incorporated, then stir in the chocolate chips. Cover and refrigerate for 30 minutes.

Preheat the oven to 170°C (325°F) Gas 3.

Now make the brownie mixture. Put the chocolate and butter in a heatproof bowl set over a pan of barely simmering water. Stir until smooth and thoroughly combined. Leave to cool slightly.

In a separate bowl, whisk the sugar, eggs and vanilla extract until pale and doubled in volume. Add the melted chocolate mixture and stir until combined. Sift the flour and salt into the bowl and fold in until well incorporated, then stir in the pecans.

Divide the brownie mixture between the prepared baking pans and spread level. Using a spoon, roughly dollop the cookie dough on top of the brownie mixture.

Place the pans on a baking sheet and bake on the middle shelf of the preheated oven for about 15 minutes, or until the cookie dough is golden brown.

Remove from the oven and leave to cool in the pans for 5 minutes, then loosen the edges of each brookie with a small palette knife. Tip the brookies out onto a wire rack and leave to cool completely.

COOKIE DOUGH

125 g/1 cup plain/all-purpose flour

½ teaspoon bicarbonate of/
   baking soda

a pinch of salt

100 g/7 tablespoons butter, softened

100 g/½ cup light muscovado/
   light brown soft sugar

50 g/¼ cup caster/granulated sugar

1 egg, lightly beaten

1 teaspoon vanilla extract

75 g/½ cup dark/bittersweet
   chocolate chips

BROWNIE MIXTURE

125 g/4 oz. dark/bittersweet
   chocolate, broken into pieces

75 g/5 tablespoons butter, cubed

125 g/⅔ cup caster/granulated
   sugar

2 eggs

1 teaspoon vanilla extract

60 g/½ cup plain/all-purpose flour

a pinch of salt

50 g/½ cup chopped pecans

10 round baking pans,
   10 cm/4 inches in diameter and
   3 cm/1 inch deep, greased and
   base lined with baking parchment

Makes 10

Brownie pops

100 g/1 cup walnuts or pecans (optional)

200 g/6½ oz. dark/bittersweet chocolate, chopped

175 g/1½ sticks butter, cubed

250 g/1¼ cups caster/granulated sugar

4 eggs

1 teaspoon vanilla extract

125 g/1 cup plain/all-purpose flour

2 tablespoons cocoa powder

a pinch of salt

75 g/½ cup milk/semisweet chocolate chips

3–4 tablespoons apricot or raspberry jam/jelly

TO DECORATE

1 quantity Milk Chocolate Topping (page 111)

assorted sugar sprinkles, stars and other edible festive decorations

a 20 x 30-cm/8 x 12-inch baking pan, greased and lined with greased baking parchment

a 5-cm/2-inch round cookie cutter

24 wooden lolly/pop sticks

Makes 24

These pops are decorated with festive Christmas sprinkles, but you can vary them according to what you are making them for. Valentine-themed pops, for example, could feature heart decorations.

It is easiest to stamp out brownie shapes if the base is prepared and baked the day before you plan to decorate your brownies.

Preheat the oven to 170°C (325°F) Gas 3.

If you're adding nuts, tip them onto a baking sheet and lightly toast in the preheated oven for 5 minutes. Roughly chop and leave to cool. Leave the oven on for the brownies.

Melt the chocolate and butter in a heatproof bowl set over a pan of barely simmering water. Do not let the base of the bowl touch the water. Stir until smooth and thoroughly combined. Leave to cool slightly.

In a separate bowl, whisk the sugar, eggs and vanilla extract with a balloon whisk until pale and thick. Add the melted chocolate mixture and stir until combined. Sift the flour, cocoa powder and salt into the bowl and fold in until well incorporated, then stir in the chocolate chips and nuts (if using). Pour the mixture into the prepared baking pan, spread level with a spatula and bake on the middle shelf of the preheated oven for 25 minutes.

Remove from the oven and leave to cool completely in the pan.

Remove the cold brownie from the pan. Using the cookie cutter, stamp out 24 rounds from the brownies and arrange on a board or tray.

Warm the jam/jelly in a small pan, sieve it, then brush it all over the brownie rounds. Leave on a wire rack for 5–10 minutes to set.

Meanwhile, prepare the Milk Chocolate Topping according to the recipe on page 111 and leave to thicken slightly.

Using a palette knife, spread the Milk Chocolate Topping evenly all over the brownie rounds, then push a lolly/pop stick into each pop. Lay them on a sheet of baking parchment and leave until the topping is starting to set. Decorate with an assortment of sprinkles and decorations by making patterns on the faces of the pops and by scattering sprinkles generously over the edges.

DELICIOUSLY DECADENT

Bijoux blondies

250 g/9 oz. white chocolate, chopped

120 g/1 stick butter, cubed

½ tablespoon sweet extra virgin olive oil

4 eggs

140 g/¾ cup caster/granulated sugar

90 g/⅔ cup plain/all-purpose flour

70 g/½ cup blanched almonds, chopped

WHITE CHOCOLATE AND OLIVE OIL GANACHE

1 vanilla pod/bean

90 ml/⅓ cup single/light cream

180 g/6½ oz. white chocolate, chopped

40 ml/3 tablespoons sweet extra virgin olive oil

blanched almonds, to decorate

a 20-cm/8-inch square baking pan, greased and lined with baking parchment

Makes 6–8

This unusual recipe uses extra virgin olive oil in the batter, which gives a deliciously tender texture to the finished blondie. For the best result, obtain a good-quality white chocolate with a low sugar content, and be sure to use fresh vanilla in the white chocolate ganache.

Preheat the oven to 170°C (325°F) Gas 3.

Melt the white chocolate and butter in a heatproof bowl set over a pan of barely simmering water. Do not let the base of the bowl touch the water. Stir occasionally until smooth. Stir in the olive oil. Remove from the heat.

In a separate bowl, whisk the eggs and sugar for 1–2 minutes. Sift in the flour and whisk again to mix. Pour the chocolate mixture in and mix well with a wooden spoon. Finally, stir in the chopped almonds.

Spoon the mixture into the prepared baking pan, spread level with a spatula and bake in the preheated oven for about 20 minutes. Allow to cool completely in the pan.

To make the white chocolate and olive oil ganache, split the vanilla pod/bean lengthways and scrape the seeds out into a pan. Add the cream and gently bring to the boil. Meanwhile, put the chocolate in a heatproof bowl set over a pan of barely simmering water. Do not let the base of the bowl touch the water. Allow to melt, stirring occasionally, until completely smooth. Add the olive oil and stir in. Remove from the heat and pour in the boiled cream. Beat with a hand-held electric whisk until smooth and glossy. Spread the ganache evenly over the cold brownie in the pan and refrigerate overnight. When you are ready to serve, cut the brownie into equal portions and decorate each one with a blanched almond.

Black forest brownies

Black cherries, Kirsch and dark/bittersweet chocolate are a classic combination. Here, black cherries preserved in a Kirsch syrup are dropped into a well-flavoured, not too sweet, brownie mixture. It makes a perfect dessert for a Christmas or New Year's party, when fruits preserved in alcohol are readily available.

Preheat the oven to 180°C (350°F) Gas 4.

Put the 225 g/8 oz. chocolate in a heatproof bowl. Add the butter and cream to the bowl and set it over a pan of barely simmering water. Melt gently, stirring frequently. Do not let the base of the bowl touch the water. Remove the bowl from the pan and set aside until needed.

Break the eggs into a mixing bowl and use a hand-held electric whisk to beat until just frothy. Add the sugar and Kirsch and beat until thick and mousse-like in texture. Whisk in the melted chocolate mixture.

Sift the flour directly onto the mixture and stir in. When thoroughly combined stir in the pieces of chocolate. Transfer the mixture to the prepared pan, spread evenly and level the surface. Gently drop the cherries onto the brownie mixture, spacing them as evenly as possible.

Bake in the preheated oven for 30–35 minutes until a skewer inserted in the middle comes out just clean. Remove the pan from the oven.

Leave to cool in the pan before removing and cutting into 24 pieces.

To serve, dust lightly with icing/confectioners' sugar and add a dollop of whipped cream on top. Store in an airtight container and eat within 4 days.

225 g/8 oz. dark/bittersweet chocolate, chopped

125 g/1⅛ sticks butter, cubed

3 tablespoons double/heavy cream

3 eggs

225 g/1 cup plus 2 tablespoons caster/granulated sugar

2 tablespoons Kirsch or Kirsch syrup from a jar of cherries

160 g/1 cup plus 3 tablespoons plain/all-purpose flour

100 g/3½ oz. dark/bittersweet chocolate, chopped, or dark choc chips

465-g/16-oz. jar black cherries in Kirsch (175 g/6 oz. drained weight)

icing/confectioners' sugar, for dusting

whipped cream, to serve

a 23-cm/9-inch square baking pan, greased and lined with baking parchment

Makes 24

Butterscotch blondies

These are a cross between blondies and brownies, with toffee, chocolate chips, nuts and a gooey caramel topping. If you can make spun sugar for decoration, all the better.

Preheat the oven to 170°C (325°F) Gas 3.

Tip the pecans onto a baking sheet and lightly toast in the preheated oven for 5 minutes. Roughly chop and leave to cool. Leave the oven on.

Sift together the flour, baking powder, bicarbonate of/baking soda and salt in a bowl.

In a separate bowl, cream together the butter and sugars until pale and light. Gradually add the eggs, beating well after each addition. Stir in the vanilla extract. Fold the sifted dry ingredients into the bowl until well incorporated, then stir in the chocolate chips, pecans and toffees. Spoon the mixture into the prepared baking pan, spread level and bake on the middle shelf of the preheated oven for 25 minutes.

Remove from the oven and leave to cool completely in the pan.

For the caramel topping, put the sugar and 1 tablespoon water in a small, heavy-based pan over low–medium heat and let the sugar dissolve without stirring. Raise the heat and continue to cook until the sugar turns a deep amber colour. Remove from the heat and add the cream – the caramel will bubble furiously and harden, but stir to melt the caramel into the cream and leave until completely cold.

Beat the butter until light and fluffy, then add the cold caramel in a steady stream and stir until thoroughly incorporated and smooth.

Remove the brownies from the pan and cut into portions. Spoon the caramel topping into the prepared piping bag and pipe a generous swirl on top of each brownie.

75 g/¾ cup pecans

225 g/1¾ cups plain/
  all-purpose flour

1 teaspoon baking powder

½ teaspoon bicarbonate of/
  baking soda

a pinch of salt

150 g/10 tablespoons butter,
  softened

150 g/¾ cup light muscovado/light
  brown soft sugar

100 g/½ cup unrefined sugar

2 eggs, lightly beaten

1 teaspoon vanilla extract

50 g/⅓ cup chocolate chips

75 g/2½ oz. toffees, chopped

CARAMEL TOPPING

150 g/¾ cup sugar

150 ml/⅔ cup double/heavy cream

200 g/1¾ sticks butter, softened

*a 20 x 30-cm/8 x 12-inch baking pan,
  greased and lined with greased
  baking parchment*

*a piping bag, fitted with a plain
  nozzle/tip*

Makes 18

Salted caramel swirl brownies

100 g/1 cup pecans

225 g/8 oz. dark/bittersweet chocolate, chopped

150 g/1 stick plus 2 tablespoons butter, cubed

225 g/1 cup caster/granulated sugar

4 eggs, lightly beaten

1 teaspoon vanilla extract

125 g/1 cup plain/all-purpose flour

a pinch of salt

SALTED CARAMEL

50 g/¼ cup caster/superfine sugar

50 g/¼ cup light muscovado/ light brown soft sugar

2 tablespoons butter

75 ml/⅓ cup double/heavy cream

½ teaspoon sea salt flakes

a 23-cm/9-inch square baking pan, greased and lined with baking parchment

Makes 25

With swirls of luscious caramel running through them, these brownies are definitely in another league. Serve cold as a quick treat or warm as a dessert, with top-notch ice cream to accompany.

Make the salted caramel first. Put the caster/superfine sugar and 2 tablespoons water in a small pan over low heat and let the sugar dissolve completely. Bring to the boil, then cook until the syrup turns to an amber-coloured caramel. Remove from the heat and add the muscovado/brown sugar, butter and cream. Stir to dissolve, then return to the low heat and simmer for 3–4 minutes until the caramel has thickened and will coat the back of a spoon. Remove from the heat, add the salt, pour into a bowl and leave until completely cold and thick.

Preheat the oven to 170°C (325°F) Gas 3.

Tip the pecans onto a baking sheet and lightly toast in the preheated oven for 5 minutes. Roughly chop and leave to cool. Leave the oven on for the brownies.

Put the chocolate and butter in a heatproof bowl set over a pan of barely simmering water. Stir until smooth and thoroughly combined. Leave to cool.

In a separate bowl, beat together the sugar, eggs and vanilla extract. Add the melted chocolate mixture and stir until combined. Sift the flour and salt into the bowl and fold in until well incorporated, then stir in the pecans.

Pour half the mixture into the prepared baking pan and spread level. Drizzle half the salted caramel over the top, then pour the remaining mixture over that. Finish by drizzling the remaining salted caramel on top, then use a round-bladed knife to swirl the mixtures together. Tap the pan on the work surface to level the mixture and bake on the middle shelf of the preheated oven for 20–25 minutes.

Remove from the oven and leave to cool completely in the pan before removing from the pan and cutting into 25 squares to serve.

Sugar and spice brownies

Aromatic cardamom and milk/semisweet chocolate are a match
made in brownie heaven - try it and love it!

100 g/3½ oz. milk/semisweet
   chocolate, chopped

200 g/1¾ sticks butter, chopped

3 pinches of ground cardamom

3 eggs

190 g/1 scant cup caster/
   granulated sugar

100 g/¾ cup plain/all-purpose
   flour

40 g/⅓ cup glacé/candied cherries,
   chopped

*a 20-cm/8-inch square baking pan,
greased and dusted with flour*

Makes 6-8

Preheat the oven to 170°C (325°F) Gas 3.

Melt the chocolate and butter in a heatproof bowl set over a pan of barely
simmering water. Do not let the base of the bowl touch the water. Stir occasionally
until very smooth. Add the cardamom and stir in with a wooden spoon. Remove
from the heat.

In a separate bowl, whisk the eggs and sugar for 1–2 minutes. Sift in the flour and
whisk again to mix. Pour the chocolate mixture in and mix well with the wooden
spoon. Finally, stir in the cherries.

Spoon the mixture into the prepared baking pan, spread level with a spatula and
bake in the preheated oven for about 25 minutes. Allow the brownies to cool in the
pan for a few minutes, then turn out onto a wire rack to cool completely. Serve at
room temperature, cut into equal portions.

Espresso brownies

This brownie is rich and fudgy with masses of chocolate, plus a good shot of strong espresso coffee to offset the sweetness. Serve with a little chilled pouring cream and you have an elegant dinner party dessert.

Preheat the oven to 180°C (350°F) Gas 4.

Melt the chocolate in a heatproof bowl set over a pan of barely simmering water. Do not let the base of the bowl touch the water. Stir occasionally until smooth. Remove the bowl from the pan and set aside until needed.

Put the soft butter and sugar in a mixing bowl and use a wooden spoon or a hand-held electric mixer to beat until light and fluffy. Gradually beat in the eggs, then the coffee.

Sift the flour and cocoa into the bowl and stir in. Add the melted chocolate and mix in. When thoroughly combined transfer the mixture to the prepared pan, spread evenly and level the surface.

Bake in the preheated oven for about 25 minutes until a skewer inserted in the middle comes out just clean. Remove the pan from the oven. Leave to cool in the pan for 10 minutes.

To serve, lightly dust with cocoa powder, remove from the pan and cut into 20 pieces. Serve warm or at room temperature with cream, if liked. Once cool, store in an airtight container and eat within 5 days.

230 g/8 oz. dark/bittersweet chocolate, chopped

115 g/1 stick butter, softened

300 g/1½ cups caster/granulated sugar

5 large eggs, lightly beaten

4 tablespoons freshly brewed strong espresso coffee, at room temperature

70 g/½ cup plain/all-purpose flour

70 g/¾ cup unsweetened cocoa powder, plus a little extra for dusting

single/light cream, to serve (optional)

a 23-cm/9-inch square baking pan, greased and lined with baking parchment

Makes 20

Half blondie, half brownie

100 g/3½ oz. dark/bittersweet chocolate, chopped

50 g/1¾ oz. white chocolate

300 g/2½ cups full-fat cream cheese

200 g/1 cup caster/granulated sugar

3 large eggs

1 teaspoon vanilla extract

100 g/¾ cup plain/all-purpose flour

100 g/¾ cup walnut pieces

a 23-cm/9-inch square baking pan, greased and lined with baking parchment

Makes 30

Incredibly rich and very moreish! This recipe uses cream cheese instead of butter and then half the mixture is flavoured with white chocolate, the rest with dark/bittersweet chocolate. Walnuts are added at the end to give a contrast in taste and texture.

Preheat the oven to 180°C (350°F) Gas 4.

Melt the dark/bittersweet chocolate in a heatproof bowl set over a pan of barely simmering water. Do not let the base of the bowl touch the water. Stir occasionally until smooth. Remove the bowl from the pan and set aside until needed. Melt the white chocolate separately in the same way and set aside to cool.

Put the cream cheese in a mixing bowl. Add the sugar and use a hand-held electric whisk to beat until smooth. Beat in the eggs, one at a time, then add the vanilla extract. Work in the flour a little at a time on low speed. Transfer half of this mixture to another bowl. Add the melted dark/bittersweet chocolate to one portion and mix thoroughly. Mix the melted white chocolate into the other portion. The dark/bittersweet chocolate mixture will be stiffer than the white.

Using a tablespoon, drop spoonfuls of the dark/bittersweet chocolate mixture into the prepared pan, spacing them evenly apart, with gaps between the blobs. Pour or spoon the white chocolate mixture over the top to fill the spaces. Scatter the nuts over the top. Use the end of a chopstick or the handle of a teaspoon to marble and swirl the two mixtures together.

Bake in the preheated oven for 25–30 minutes until a skewer inserted in the middle comes out just clean. Leave to cool in the pan before removing and cutting into 30 small pieces. Store in an airtight container and eat within 5 days.

These dark, double-chocolate brownies have a light texture and are subtly flavoured with rum. Serve warm or at room-temperature with a scoop of vanilla ice cream and hot creamy chocolate sauce for a deliciously grown-up dessert.

Choc choc rum brownies

60 g/2 oz. dark/bittersweet chocolate, chopped

85 g/6 tablespoons butter, softened

200 g/scant 1½ cups icing/confectioners' sugar

2 large eggs, lightly beaten

2 tablespoons dark rum

60 g/scant ½ cup plain/all-purpose flour

100 g/3½ oz. dark/bittersweet chocolate, finely chopped or dark chocolate chips

50 g/¼ cup walnut pieces

CREAMY CHOCOLATE SAUCE

125 ml/½ cup double/heavy cream

75 g/2½ oz. dark/bittersweet chocolate (60–70% cocoa solids), chopped

½ teaspoon vanilla extract

vanilla ice cream, to serve

a 23-cm/9-inch square baking pan, greased and lined with baking parchment

Makes 16

Preheat the oven to 180°C (350°F) Gas 4.

Melt the 60 g/2 oz. chocolate in a heatproof bowl set over a pan of barely simmering water. Do not let the base of the bowl touch the water. Stir occasionally until smooth. Remove the bowl from the pan and set aside until needed.

Put the soft butter and icing/confectioners' sugar in a mixing bowl and beat with a wooden spoon or hand-held electric whisk until light and creamy.

Gradually beat in the eggs, followed by the rum. Scrape down the sides of the bowl then beat in the melted chocolate. Stir in the flour, and when thoroughly combined, add the chopped chocolate and the nuts and mix thoroughly. Transfer the mixture to the prepared pan, spread evenly and level the surface with the back of a spoon.

Bake in the preheated oven for about 20–25 minutes until the top is set and firm. Leave to cool a little in the pan before removing (taking care as the crust is fragile) and cutting into 16 pieces.

To make the creamy chocolate sauce, pour the cream into a small heavy-based pan and heat gently, stirring frequently. When the cream comes to the boil remove the pan from the heat and let cool for a minute. Stir in the chocolate pieces and vanilla and keep stirring until the sauce is smooth. Transfer into a warmed jug/pitcher and pour over the brownies and ice cream to serve.

The sauce will thicken as it cools but can be gently reheated, and the brownies will keep in an airtight container at room temperature for 4 days.

The supreme brownie

225 g/8 oz. dark/bittersweet
    chocolate (55% cocoa
    solids), chopped

200 g/1¾ sticks butter,
    cubed

4 eggs

130 g/⅔ cup caster/
    granulated sugar

125 g/1 scant cup plain/
    all-purpose flour

SYRUP

1 vanilla pod/bean

finely grated zest of
    ½ orange

finely grated zest of
    ½ lemon

¼ teaspoon ground
    cinnamon

¼ teaspoon ground nutmeg

50 g/¼ cup caster/superfine
    sugar

50 ml/¼ cup Irish cream
    liqueur (such as Baileys)

*a 20-cm/8-inch square baking
    pan, greased and dusted
    with flour*

Makes 6-8

Supreme by name, supreme by taste. If you are looking for a dessert-style brownie with the wow-factor to impress guests, this might be the one for you. The whiskey liqueur syrup adds a caramel sweetness offset by the orange and lemon zest, cinnamon and nutmeg. Pouring the syrup over the brownie will allow it to seep in and turn it into more of a sticky dessert.

Preheat the oven to 170°C (325°F) Gas 3.

Melt the chocolate and butter in a heatproof bowl set over a pan of barely simmering water. Do not let the base of the bowl touch the water. Stir occasionally until very smooth. Remove from the heat.

In a separate bowl, whisk the eggs and sugar for 1–2 minutes. Sift in the flour and whisk again to mix. Pour the chocolate mixture in and mix well with a wooden spoon.

Spoon the mixture into the prepared baking pan, spread level with the back of a spoon and bake in the preheated oven for about 25 minutes. Remove from the oven and leave in the baking pan while you make the Baileys syrup.

To make the syrup, split the vanilla pod/bean lengthways and scrape the seeds out into a small pan. Add the citrus zest, cinnamon, nutmeg, sugar and 50 ml/¼ cup cold water and gently bring to the boil. Stir in the Irish cream liqueur.

Brush the syrup evenly over the warm brownie in the pan, using a pastry brush, then allow to cool.

Serve at room temperature, cut into equal portions.

Chilli pecan brownies

Containing coriander seeds, cardamom, cinnamon, nutmeg and black pepper (among other spices), Baharat spice blend is a perfect spicy addition to add to any dark/bittersweet chocolate dish. Leftover caramelized nuts can also be served on their own as a sweet nibble or to finish a meal with a full-bodied coffee.

Preheat the oven to 180°C (350°F) Gas 4.

To make the caramelized chilli pecans, put 50 ml/3 tablespoons water and the sugar in a small frying pan/skillet over medium heat and stir with a wooden spatula for 2 minutes. Add the pecans and stir well as the water evaporates. After 3–4 minutes, add the chilli powder/ground chile and salt, stirring all the time and making sure the pecans are evenly coated. Continue stirring for a few minutes longer until all the water has evaporated, the pecans are coated and the pan is dry. Tip the pecans onto a plate or waxed paper to cool.

To make the brownies, melt the chocolate and butter in a heatproof bowl set over a pan of barely simmering water. Do not let the base of the bowl touch the water. Stir occasionally until smooth then let cool for a few minutes. Add the sugar and mix to combine.

Beat the eggs and vanilla into the chocolate mixture in the pan with the wooden spoon until well blended. Sift the flour, Baharat spice blend and salt into the pan and stir until just mixed. Stir in the caramelized pecans.

Pour the batter into the prepared baking pan, spreading evenly. Bake in the preheated oven for 25–30 minutes until firm or until a skewer inserted into the middle comes out clean. Let cool in the baking pan on a wire rack, then cut the brownies into squares. They should keep for 1 week stored in an airtight container.

Note: Baharat is a Middle Eastern ingredient available online and in larger stores. The spices it contains may vary from region to region but it usually contains the following: paprika, coriander, black pepper, cumin, cinnamon, cayenne pepper, cloves, nutmeg and cardamom. You can substitute the same amount of mixed spice/apple pie spice and a pinch of cayenne pepper.

100 g/3½ oz. dark/bittersweet (75% cocoa solids) chocolate, chopped

125 g/1 stick butter, cubed

250 g/1¼ cups caster/superfine sugar

3 large eggs, lightly beaten

1 teaspoon vanilla extract

200 g/1⅔ cups plain/all-purpose flour

2 teaspoons Baharat spice blend (see Note)

a pinch of salt

CARAMELIZED CHILLI PECANS

2 tablespoons caster/superfine sugar

100 g/⅔ cup chopped pecans

1 teaspoon hot chilli powder/ground red chile

a pinch of salt

a 23 x 33-cm/9 x 13-inch baking pan, greased and lined with baking parchment

Makes 12

Bacon, maple and pecan brownies

12 rashers/slices smoked
streaky bacon, finely
chopped

75 g/¼ cup maple syrup

250 g/8 oz. dark/bittersweet
chocolate (60–70% cocoa
solids), chopped

250 g/2 sticks butter

125 g/⅔ cup light
muscovado/light brown
soft sugar

125 g/⅔ cup caster/
granulated sugar

4 eggs, beaten

a pinch of salt

100 g/¾ cup plain/
all-purpose flour

½ teaspoon baking powder

½ teaspoon bicarbonate of/
baking soda

100 g/⅔ cup pecans, roughly
chopped

**MISO CARAMEL
VARIATION**

175 g/¾ cup plus 2
tablespoons caster/
granulated sugar

125 ml/½ cup double/
heavy cream

2 tablespoons white miso

2 teaspoons vanilla extract

*a 20 x 25-cm/8 x 10-inch
baking pan, greased
and lined with baking
parchment*

Makes 16

The heady combination of salt and sweet makes these bacon, maple and pecan brownies irresistibly seductive. Or, for a meat-free alternative, try the umami-rich and gloriously sticky chocolate and miso caramel variation.

Preheat the oven to 170°C (325°F) Gas 3.

First, dry fry the bacon in a frying pan/skillet set over a medium heat until golden. Stir in the maple syrup, turn off the heat and set aside to cool in the pan.

Melt the chocolate and butter in a heatproof bowl set over a pan of barely simmering water. Do not let the base of the bowl touch the water. Stir occasionally until smooth. Take the bowl off the heat and leave to cool slightly before whisking in the sugars, bacon syrup, eggs and salt. Sift in the flour and raising agents, and fold in together with the pecans.

Pour the mixture into the prepared pan and bake in the preheated oven for 25–30 minutes, or until just set. A skewer inserted into the middle should still have a little stickiness left on it. Remove from the oven and let cool in the pan on top of a wire rack before turning out and cutting into squares.

Chocolate brownies with miso caramel:

For a miso caramel variation of these brownies, omit the bacon, maple syrup and pecans and begin by making the caramel. Put the sugar and 70 ml/⅓ cup of water in a pan set over a gentle heat and stir until the sugar has dissolved. Stop stirring, increase the heat and bring the syrup to the boil. Use a wet pastry brush to wash down any sugar crystals that stick to the side of the pan. When the sugar turns deep amber, remove from the heat and carefully pour in the cream. The mixture will bubble up, but whisk well to mix. If the cold cream causes the caramel to harden too much, pop it back over a gentle heat until it melts again. Whisk in the miso and set aside.

As above, make the brownie mixture but add vanilla with the salt.

Pour the mixture into the prepared pan and level the top with the back of a spoon. Drizzle over half of the miso caramel. If the miso caramel has hardened, gently heat it to soften it again. Use a skewer to swirl the caramel around and bake as above.

Remove from the oven and immediately drizzle the rest of the caramel over the top. Leave to cool in the pan, turn out and cut as above.

Moonies

250 g/8 oz. dark/bittersweet chocolate, chopped

125 g/1 stick butter

¼ teaspoon salt

125 g/⅔ cup light muscovado sugar/light brown soft sugar

125 g/⅔ cup caster/granulated sugar

4 eggs, beaten

75 g/⅔ cup rice flour

50 g/⅓ cup plus 1 tablespoon unsweetened cocoa powder

1 teaspoon baking powder

MOUSSE FILLING

150 g/5 oz. dark/bittersweet chocolate, chopped

55 g/½ cup icing/confectioners' sugar

100 g/6½ tablespoons butter

3 large eggs, separated

a pinch of salt

90 ml/⅓ cup plus 1 tablespoon double/heavy cream

2 x 20-cm/8-inch square cake pans, greased and lined with baking parchment

Makes 16

A mash-up between mousse and brownie, these moonies offer so much more than just a silly name. Rich and silky chocolate mousse is sandwiched between two layers of sticky brownie. This treat will be sure to transform your afternoon cake fix from the mundane to something spectacular.

Preheat the oven to 160°C (325°F) Gas 3.

Melt the chocolate and butter with the salt in a heatproof bowl set over a pan of barely simmering water. Do not let the base of the bowl touch the water. Stir occasionally until smooth. Once melted, stir in the sugars. Remove the bowl from the heat and mix in the eggs. Sift over the flour, cocoa and baking powder and mix together. Divide the mixture between the prepared cake pans. Level the top with a palette knife and bake for 20–25 minutes. A skewer inserted into the middle should still have a little stickiness left on it. Leave to cool in the cake pans on top of a wire rack before turning out.

To make the mousse filling, melt the chocolate in a heatproof bowl set over a pan of barely simmering water. Do not let the base of the bowl touch the water. Once melted, take the chocolate off the heat and stir in the butter until melted.

Whisk in the egg yolks, one at a time, until fully incorporated. Sift over the icing/confectioners' sugar and mix in. In a spotlessly clean bowl and with a clean hand-held electric whisk, beat the egg whites with the salt to stiff peaks. Set aside while you whisk the cream to stiff peaks.

Fold the cream into the chocolate mixture. Next, fold in the egg whites using a large metal spoon. Place one of the cold brownies inside a deep cake pan (preferably with a loose-bottom) of the same size. Pour the mousse over the top and level it over with the back of a spoon. Finally, place the other brownie on top and put the cake pan in the fridge to chill for at least 8 hours (or overnight).

Run a knife around the edges of the cake pan, before taking the moonie out of its pan. Carefully slice into 16 squares.

1 tablespoon butter, melted

1 tablespoon plain/all-purpose flour

1 quantity Deep Dark Chocolate
Brownie (page 82)

TO DECORATE

150 g/5½ oz. white chocolate, chopped

1 quantity Ganache Topping (page 25)

3–4 tablespoons apricot or
raspberry jam/jelly

red liquid food colouring

red or pink edible glitter

red heart-shaped sugar sprinkles

*a baking sheet, lined with
baking parchment*

*12 heart-shaped baking pans measuring
10 cm/4 inches across, base lined
with baking parchment (if you don't
have as many as 12 pans, just bake
the hearts in batches)*

a clean toothbrush

*small heart-shaped cookie cutters
in various sizes*

Makes 12

Love heart brownies

Make the white chocolate hearts in advance and refrigerate until
needed. To continue the theme, look out for heart-shaped sugar
sprinkles in bakeware stores or from online suppliers.

Start by making the white chocolate hearts, to decorate. Melt the white
chocolate in a heatproof bowl set over a pan of barely simmering water. Do not
let the base of the bowl touch the water. Stir occasionally until smooth. Pour the
chocolate onto the prepared baking sheet and spread evenly to a thickness of
2 mm/¹⁄₁₆ inch. Leave in a cool place to set completely.

Preheat the oven to 170°C (325°F) Gas 3.

Lightly brush the insides of the heart-shaped pans with the melted butter and
line the bases with a piece of greased baking parchment. Now dust the insides of
the pans with the flour and tip out the excess.

Prepare the Deep Dark Chocolate Brownie mixture according to the recipe
on page 82 and divide between the prepared baking pans. (If you don't have
12 pans, you will need to bake the hearts in batches.) Arrange on a baking sheet
and cook on the middle shelf of the preheated oven for about 12–15 minutes.

Remove from the oven and leave to cool in the pans for 10 minutes before
turning out onto a wire rack to cool completely.

Meanwhile, prepare the Ganache Topping according to the recipe on
page 25. Warm the jam/jelly in a small pan, strain away any seeds, then brush
it over the tops of the brownies. Leave to set for 5 minutes.

Trickle a little red food colouring onto a saucer, then dip the clean
toothbrush into it. Flick the bristles over half the slab of set white chocolate
so that it is flecked with red. Sprinkle edible glitter over the remainder of the
chocolate and leave to dry, then stamp out hearts with the cookie cutters.

Spread the Chocolate Ganache over the tops of the brownies and decorate
with the white chocolate hearts and sugar sprinkles.

Index

Picture credits

Food photography by the following:

Carolyn Barber
Page 14

Martin Brigdale
Pages 30, 69

Peter Cassidy
Pages 2, 66, 86, 91, 98, 99, 108, 135, 150

Laura Edwards
Pages 4, 6–7, 24, 32, 33, 43, 74, 80, 83, 107, 109, 110, 114–115, 118, 119, 122, 123, 126, 128, 129, 137, 138, 157

Tara Fisher
Pages 116 insert, 117

Jonathan Gregson
Pages 8, 17 insert, 56, 60, 77 insert, 104, 120, 130, 132, 134, endpapers

Dan Jones
Pages 40, 153

Richard Jung
Pages 1, 5 insert, 13, 38 insert, 68, 72, 79, 142, 143, 145, 146

William Lingwood
Page 116 background

Steve Painter
Pages 3, 5 background, 9-11, 15, 18–21, 31, 36, 37, 45–47, 49, 50, 53, 54, 62, 70, 71, 73 background, 96, 97, 112–113, 121, 127 insert, 131, 133, 136, 141, 148, 149

William Reavell
Pages 51, 73 insert, 85, 87, 102, 103, 105, 139, 151

Kate Whitaker
Pages 12, 28, 29, 34–35, 38-39 background, 42, 48, 52, 55, 57–59, 63–65, 78, 84, 88, 92, 95, 100-101, 106, 140, 144, 156, 160

Isobel Wield
Pages 16, 23, 27, 44, 67, 75, 76, 127 background

Clare Winfield
Pages 17 background, 41, 89, 90, 93, 94, 124, 125, 154

Recipe credits

Amy Ruth Finegold
Apricot flax oat bars
Carrot oat squares
Cocoa energy bars
Ginger cashew granola bars

Annie Rigg
Apricot and almond brownies
Brookies
Brownie pops
Brownie whoopie pies
Butterscotch blondies
Coffee blondies
Double white chocolate and pecan blondies
Fudge crumble brownies
Gingerbread brownies
Hazelnut praline brownies
Love heart brownies

Malted milk chocolate traybake
Mint chocolate chip brownies
Peanut butter and jelly brownies
Salted caramel swirl brownies

Bea Vo
Belgian blondies
Lavender shortbread

Carol Hilker
Chocolate marshmallow brownies

Claire Burnet
Very berry cheesecake brownies

Dan May
Chilli pecan brownies

Hannah Miles
Gluten-free coconut and pumpkin power bars
Rocky road popcorn slice

Jordan Bourke
Orange zest brownies

Laura Washburn
Apple, fig and nut bars

Julian Day
Bakewell slices
Chocolate fudge brownies
Chocolate tiffin
Chocolate, ginger and orange slice
Flapjacks
Maggie's muesli bars
Parkin pieces

Nicola Graimes
Summer fruit slice

Linda Collister
Black forest brownies
Choc choc rum brownies
Cinnamon pecan blondies
Coconut blondies
Espresso brownies
Extra-nutty brownies
Flourless sticky brownies
Half blondie half brownie
Macadamia and white chocolate blondies

Liz Franklin
Banana and nutmeg custard brownies
Buttery carrot cake
Fudgy dark chocolate and almond traybake
Pistachio brownies

Mickael Benichou
Bijoux blondies

Bonjour brownies
Crackling brownie French fries
Sugar and spice brownies
The supreme brownie

Sarah Randell
Cherry marzipan streusel squares
Chocolate fudge raspberry shortbread bars
Coconut, apricot and lime slices
Honey, toasted pine nut and pumpkin-seed flapjacks with chocolate topping
Lemon squares
Nectarine and blueberry traybake with lavender sugar
Sticky toffee traybake with toffee fudge drizzle

Shelagh Ryan
Spiced pear cake

Victoria Glass
Bacon, maple and pecan brownies
Chocolate and hazelnut brownies
Millionaire's shortbread
Millionairejacks
Moonies
White chocolate and blueberry blondies

Will Torrent
Cranberry and white chocolate blondies